OPIUM CITY

# OPIUM CITY

## THE MAKING OF
## EARLY VICTORIAN BOMBAY

AMAR FAROOQUI

**Three Essays**
COLLECTIVE

First Edition January 2006

Fifth Printing August 2022
copyright ©Three Essays, 2006. All rights reserved

ISBN 978-81-88789-42-9

**Three Essays**
COLLECTIVE

B 957, Palam Vihar, Gurgaon 122 017 India
Phone:  0 98681 26587, 0 98683 44843
info@threeessays.com   Website: www.threeessays.com
Printed at Chaman Offset Printers, New Delhi

For
Sehba

# ACKNOWLEDGEMENTS

I am thankful to the Charles Wallace India Trust and the Indian Council of Historical Research for providing me with financial assistance to visit repositories in UK. I wish to express my gratitude to Matheson and Co., London, for permission to consult the Jardine Matheson Archives at the University Library, Cambridge.

I am indebted to Sharit Bhowmik for making it possible for me to undertake several trips to Mumbai, to Biswamoy Pati who lent constant encouragement, and Asad Zaidi who made this book possible.

I would like to acknowledge the help given to me by librarians, archivists and other staff of the several institutions where I carried out research for this book: the National Archives of India, Nehru Memorial Museum and Library, Maharashtra State Archives, Goa State Archives, Xavier Centre for Historical Research, British Library, and Cambridge University Library.

The first and third essays include revised versions of some parts of my article 'Urban Development in a Colonial Situation: Early Nineteenth Century Bombay', published in *Economic and Political Weekly*, Vol. XXXI, no. 40, 1996.

# CONTENTS

Because India cannot fill up the remorseless Drain, so China must be dragged in to make it up, even though it be being 'poisoned'... This opium trade is a sin on England's head, and a curse on India for her share in being the instrument.

Dadabhai Naoroji, 1880

# INTRODUCTION

At the beginning of the nineteenth century Bombay was still, as it had been since the middle of the seventeenth century when it came into the possession of the East India Company, a relatively minor British outpost on the west coast of India. Its transformation into one of the leading cities of the empire occurred fairly rapidly within the space of about four decades during the first half of the nineteenth century. Circa 1800-1840 Bombay became a major exporter of opium and raw cotton, mainly to China. The role played by these two commodities in the rise of Bombay and its capitalist class is generally recognized,[1] but the centrality of opium has not been sufficiently emphasized.

Moreover, the structure of the opium trade in relation to the colonial economy of Bombay remains imperfectly understood. The only detailed, though by no means exhaustive, account of the subject is Asiya Siddiqi's article 'The Business World of Jamsetjee Jejeebhoy' published in 1982.[2] In fact as John F. Richards has recently remarked, 'South Asian historians are just beginning to address the complexities of the opium industry in India'.[3] Siddiqi's seminal paper, which has established itself as a classic, revealed the inner mechanism of the trade, underlined the importance of opium for capital accumulation in Bombay, and brought out vividly the limitations of indigenous participation in a venture that was ultimately designed to serve British interests. Her analysis, based on the extensive information available in letterbooks of the prominent opium exporter Jamsetjee Jejeebhoy, confirmed that the commodity was crucial for the networks that sustained the 'business world' of Bombay.

The present essays attempt to explore the linkages between the opium trade and the creation of early Victorian Bombay. They outline the development of the port as a colonial urban centre against the backdrop of trafficking in the drug. Opium was the defining feature of the economic world of Bombay and its business class. This class had grown to maturity by the 1830s. The Bombay Chamber of Commerce, which included several Indian firms, was founded in 1836—a year before Victoria ascended the throne.

The term 'early Victorian' is used essentially in a chronological sense, while at the same time bearing in mind that the use of urban space and the evolution of architectural styles were determined by the experience of cities of Victorian Britain. Victorian attitudes and values also conditioned the cultural milieu of the indigenous elite of Bombay in very specific ways, as for instance the 'westernization' of the Parsi business class. To quote Asa Briggs, 'In social texture as well as in architecture Bombay belonged unmistakably to Queen Victoria's world'.[4]

Early Victorian Bombay was a pre-industrial city, a city of the pre-railway era. Large parts of it were semi-urban, or even rural, in appearance. It did not yet have a municipal corporation. The imposing and exotic buildings which were to dot its skyline by the end of the century had not been constructed. But it had a brisk long-distance shipping trade, a thriving dockyard, and large scale commercial and financial activity. Indian business had a strong presence in the city. The diverse composition of the capitalist class in terms of the communities from which it was drawn – Parsi, Marwari, Konkani Muslim, Gujarati Bania, Bohra, Armenian, Indo-Portuguese, to name only a few—gave it a cosmopolitan character, which was reinforced by a relatively high degree of collaboration with private European traders.[5] The openness that this implied rendered Bombay less of a Maharashtrian and more of an imperial city. We can locate herein the roots of that process which enabled Bombay to become the main centre of Indian cinema in the post-independence period, a cinema that could communicate in a national idiom giving to it an all-India appeal.[6]

The first essay deals with the problems of early colonial Bombay that were responsible for its relative obscurity till the end of the eighteenth century. There was a distinct possibility even in the last quarter of the eighteenth century that the settlement might be downgraded to the status of a small commercial establishment even though it had an excellent harbour. Maintaining a large administrative apparatus for governing the city was an expensive proposition for the East India Company since Bombay was unable to sustain itself financially. Opium and raw cotton completely altered this situation and by the turn of the century the company was looking forward to the substantial benefits that the port now seemed capable of yielding. The second essay discusses the place of opium in the network of commercial and economic relationships of Bombay in the early nineteenth century. Opium, especially Malwa opium, played a pivotal role in integrating Bombay with the west coast of India, Rajasthan, Sind and Malwa, as well as with China. It was primarily opium that linked Bombay to the international capitalist economy. This was also the time when Bombay became the main commercial and financial centre of western India. The emergence of an indigenous capitalist class centred on the port can be directly traced to the participation of Indian business groups in the opium enterprise and the profits they earned from it. The third essay outlines some of the prominent features of urban development in Bombay during the early Victorian era, and how these reflect the collaboration and conflict that characterized the relationship between the capitalist class of the city and British colonial rule.

## Notes

[1] Cf. Amalendu Guha, 'Parsi Seths as Entrepreneurs: 1750-1850', *EPW*, Vol. V, 35 (1970), pp. M 107-115; and 'Comprador Role of Parsi Seths: 1750-1850', *EPW*, Vol. V, 48 (1970), pp.1933-1936.

[2] Asiya Siddiqi, 'The Business World of Jamsetjee Jejeebhoy', *IESHR*, Vol. XIX, 3 and 4 (1982), reprinted in Asiya Siddiqi (ed.), *Trade and Finance in Colonial India, 1750-1860* (Delhi, 1985), pp.186-217 (all references are to the article reproduced in this volume).

[3] John F. Richards, 'The Opium Industry in British India', *IESHR*, Vol. XXXIX, 2 and 3 (2002), p.152.

[4] Asa Briggs, *Victorian Cities* (Harmondsworth, 1977), pp.277-278.

[5] Christine Dobbin's major social and intellectual history of nineteenth century Bombay, *Urban Leadership in Western India: Politics and Communities in Bombay City, 1840-1885* (London, 1972), which is concerned with the period from the 1840s onwards, contains valuable insights on the antecedents of the Bombay shetias and its opening chapter is devoted entirely to the business groups of the city during the early nineteenth century.

[6] This is not to ignore the contribution of leftwing counter-culture of the twentieth century (of which Bombay was a major centre and its cinema an important vehicle) in developing such an idiom. It is also not surprising that the most organized rightwing political force in contemporary Bombay, the Shiv Sena, has consistently stood for anti-cosmopolitanism. Ever since its rise in the late 1960s the Sena has promoted its extreme rightwing and rabidly communal politics by insisting upon an exclusively Maharashtrian identity for Bombay/Mumbai.

# BOMBAY: A COLONIAL PORT
# IN SEARCH OF BUSINESS

Bombay island is one of a group of about twenty-five islands lying off the Konkan coast of western India, separated from the mainland by the Thane creek and Harbour Bay.[1] Apart from Bombay this group of islands includes Salsette, the large nothern neighbour of Bombay. Bombay in turn consists of seven islands, namely, Colaba and Old Woman's Island (also known as Lower Colaba) at the southern extremity; Mazagaon; Worli; Mahim and Parel (Sion-Wadala-Sewri) in the north; and in the centre the large H-shaped island Bombay, which eventually lent its name to the entire group (see Map 1).[2] Over the years these islands have been united by causeways and breakwaters so that today one would not be aware that in going from the Gateway of India to the Asiatic Society Library one had traversed over Colaba and Old Woman's Island.

Bombay possesses from the safety of its port a distinct advantage. It has a harbour with an effective area of about 194 sq km of shallowed deep water, making it one of the most suitable places along the west coast of India for receiving and putting out ships.[3]

The 'Vasco da Gama era' of Bombay's history began with the arrival of the Portuguese on the island in 1509 and the establishment of their authority over it in 1534.[4] Details of the early colonial history of the city are well-known and need not detain us. Suffice it to say that the Portuguese made over Bombay to the British under the provisions of the treaty of 1661 concluded on the occasion of the marriage of Charles II of Great Britain and Catherine Braganza of Portugal.[5] The British crown got actual possession of the island in 1665, and in turn handed it over to the East India Company for a token £10 annual rent.[6]

Bombay as an urban centre is a British creation. It does not have much of a pre-colonial past. The subsequent greatness of the city should not tempt us to think in terms of the inevitability of its rise. True, Bombay possesses from the safety of its port a distinct advantage which was crucial to its emergence as a major commercial centre. However, Bombay has not always been very easily accessible from the surrounding parts of western and central India. For one, the Sahyadri mountains act as a barrier between the coast and the Deccan tableland.[7] The relative inaccessibility of Bombay from western and central India was reflected in its peripheral position in the context of the commercial network of the area well into the nineteenth century. In the middle of the nineteenth century when a railway network for western and central India with Bombay as its focal point was being contemplated, attention was drawn to the fact that the country to be traversed in going from western and central India to Bombay was 'intersected by no navigable stream' and did not have 'any of the facilities which good roads afford';[8] and dwelling on some of the drawbacks of the city's position, the *Bombay Times* noted that 'Bombay unlike Calcutta, is not situated on the estuary of a hundred rivers, and that its less favoured inhabitants have no rich alluvial plains like those watered by the Ganges, nor roads such as they have in Bengal'.[9]

While the favourable situation of Bombay along the western coast equipped it for its development as a port, the geographical relationship of Bombay with western (and central) India was not a very close one. Few overland trade routes were directed towards Bombay. In fact down to the eighteenth century the main overland routes linking northern and central India with the Arabian sea terminated almost 300 kilometers north of Bombay. The Gulf of Khambat (Cambay) was the main catchment area for goods flowing towards the west coast for overseas shipment.[10] Khambat, Bharuch, Jambusar, Daman and Diu, and above all Surat, were the destinations of caravans arriving from Agra, Ahmadabad, Burhanpur, Navsari, Sironj, Ujjain, etc.[11] A minor route, running south of Surat, stopped short of Bombay at Bassein.[12] On the Konkan coast, Chaul, Dabhol and Vengurla supplied merchandise to Surat but the trade remained essentially coastal,[13] the Konkan till very recently being relatively inaccessible by overland transport. To the east of Bombay, the western ghats prevented the interior of Maharashtra from being easily converted into a hinterland for Bombay. Consequently, Bombay was only a getting-off point for coastal trade and not a destination for overland routes. The insularity of Bombay was completed by (a) the fact that it was an island that was not adequately integrated with the mainland, and (b) possession by the Marathas, till the 1770s, of adjoining Salsette.

Bombay was dependent on sea-borne trade even for its basic necessities. This contributed to enhancing the extrovert character of Bombay's economy from the time of British occupation. When Bombay came into the company's possession only a small portion of the island was in a state of cultivation.[14] John Burnell, writing during the first decade of the eighteenth century made the following observation about the supply of food to the island:[15]

> Cows are a scarce commodity on the Island, as in truth is every thing else of provision, we being beholden to our neighbours the Portugueze [sic] for almost every thing that we eat; otherwise we might starve, were we only to subsist on the production of the Island.

Though in decline, the Portuguese presence on the west coast was still quite visible in the early eighteenth century as is indicated by, among other things, 'the role of the Portuguese language as the lingua franca of all commercial intercourse in which Europeans took part'.[16] What is significant is that Bombay's reliance on the residual commerce of the Portuguese for providing its inhabitants with articles of subsistence underscored the island's coastal and hence extrovert nature.

Moreover, the unassailable position of Surat as a major centre of foreign trade along the western coast of India for most of the seventeenth and part of the eighteenth century precluded the possibility of fully utilizing the potential of Bombay. Yet, the decline of Surat by the middle of the eighteenth century did not immediately open up opportunities for Bombay. The initial growth of the city was slow and arduous. It is necessary to stand back a little and locate the problems of Bombay within the larger picture of western India rather than view them within the limited context of Bombay/Surat alone.

It would not be sufficient to talk in terms of the competition offered by Surat since the decline of Surat did not, and could not, by itself be the starting point of Bombay's rise. The factors leading to the decline of Surat were, after all, not specific to that city alone. They influenced the trade and economy of the north-western coast of India in general. Ashin Das Gupta's masterly study of the circumstances which led to a reversal in the fortunes of Surat has shifted the focus from reasons like the silting of river Tapti (on which Surat is situated),[17] or the sack of the city by Shivaji in 1664 and 1670, traditionally suggested to explain its decline.[18] Das Gupta has argued that the decline of the city was the result of a particular conjuncture: the almost simultaneous waning of three great empires which had contributed to the immense prosperity of Surat in the first place – the Mughal empire in India, the Safavid empire in Iran and the Ottoman empire in the West Asia.[19] The Red Sea and the Persian Gulf had become increasingly important for Surat merchants. The weakening of Safavid and Ottoman authority disrupted Surat's trade with West Asia. More crucial was the decline of the Mughals during the early eighteenth century.

Das Gupta has drawn attention to the adverse impact of the instability of the opening years of the eighteenth century on the economic activity of western India, and of Gujarat in particular. Political upheavals of the period brought to an end 'Mughal peace' and led to tremendous insecurity. Long-distance overland trade links which had given Surat access to distant centres like Agra, Lahore, Banaras etc., were suddenly broken.[20]

The large canvas within which Das Gupta has placed the decline of Surat allows us to see this phenomenon as one that was part of a general crisis in western Indian trade. If Surat, around which the economic life of the north-western coast of India had revolved, failed to survive, could Bombay, with its peripheral geographical and economic position, be expected to make a sudden impact?[21]

Bombay's coastal trade, which was largely in English hands, was also facing problems arising out of a shift during the first half of the eighteenth century in the focus of English commercial activities in India from the west to the east; to the Coromondal and thence to Bengal.[22] By the 1740s, while there was on the one had an increase in Bengal's Europe trade, with piece-goods, raw silk and saltpetre as the main commodities, on the other hand there was a downward trend in the Europe trade of Bombay and Surat.[23] Decline in the demand for indigo, an item which had hitherto been important in the English East India Company's import list, further contributed to the eclipse of Surat's Europe trade.[24] From the 1740s onwards trade between the west and east coast of India too tended to get neglected.[25] Holden Furber linked this decline of sea-borne trade between the east coast and the west coast to a 'commercial revolution' in the mid-eighteenth century 'when the conquests and rivalries of European powers fostered a rapid expansion of trade between India and China'.[26]

Ultimately it was this very 'commercial revolution' which gave to Bombay its great chance. There is, however, the very crucial question of timing, both of the expansion of Bengal's eastward trade as well as that of the rise of Bombay. P.J. Marshall in his study of private British trade in Bengal has gone along with Furber in regarding the west coast trade to be in decline by the 1740s[27]— a point on which many of the writings of the last few decades on the subject are generally in agreement.[28] However, while Furber had spoken of the almost simultaneous decline of western trade and growth of eastern trade,[29] Marshall has suggested that the 'eastward trade was not providing substantial compensations until the 1770s',[30] i.e., that there was a gap of about 'thirty barren years' between the two developments.[31]

It might be useful to note this thirty year gap in the context of Bombay's rise. If one understands the inability of Bombay to take advantage of the decline of Surat as being the outcome of (i) a general crisis of the western Indian trade network caused by the decline of the Mughal, Safavid and Ottoman empires; (ii) decline in the Europe trade of India's west coast and (iii) Bengal's shift away from trade with the west coast; or in other words, the result of problems afflicting the foreign trade of western India as a whole, so that it would not be immediately possible for Bombay to race ahead at the cost of Surat, we must then allow some time for a new set of circumstances which could help Bombay to realize its potential to emerge. There was a lag, as Marshall observes, in the case of Bengal, where, by the eighteenth century, most of the activities of the English East India Company were already centred. The lag was much more in the case of Bombay, which had to build its trading network and its spatial relationship with a hinterland almost from the scratch, as it were.

As late as 1788 Lord Cornwallis found it incomprehensible that a huge establishment should be maintained at Bombay, 'to load one ship in the year and to collect a very small revenue'.[32] He noted with dismay that the company had 'appropriated the whole surplus revenue of Benaras and Bahar [sic] to the support of Bombay', and yet was 'obliged to send many lacs thither from Calcutta'.[33] Cornwallis therefore recommended that Bombay be demoted to the position of 'just a small factory'.[34] Writing to William Pitt he declared: 'I have reflected most seriously, and have conversed with the most sensible men in this country, on the utility of the civil establishment at Bombay and I am perfectly convinced that the Company derive no benefit from it'.[35] He ruefully added that, 'I see two material obstacles to the abolition of it: the unwillingness of the Court of Directors to lose the appointment of so many writers, and the difficulty of overcoming prejudice and ancient habits'.[36] Bombay was thus still struggling to survive in the closing years of the eighteenth century.

Pamela Nightingale has suggested that the period after 1784 was critical for Bombay's 'take-off'.[37] In 1784 Bombay's trade received a boost with the rise, she argues, in raw cotton exports to China. These were to pay for the English East India Company's increased purchases of Chinese tea, which in turn grew by leaps and bounds following Pitt's Commutation Act of 1784 which lowered the duty on tea.[38] Although there is no denying the significant role of raw cotton in the Bombay-China trade, a little circumspection is called for in regarding cotton as the commodity responsible for Bombay's breakthrough.[39] Raw cotton exports from India to China increased steadily but the search for the right commodity with which to exchange tea was far from complete. Raw cotton exports were not able to keep pace with import of tea from China.

The solution was eventually provided by opium, particularly in the 1820s when exports of opium from eastern India, which had already been rising constantly since the end of the eighteenth century, combined with large exports of opium from western India as well. This period saw a quantum leap in the value of opium imports into China (see Table 1).

One would like to suggest that the rise of Bombay coincided with an opium 'miracle', and consequently that it would be appropriate to move forward the date of Bombay's ascendancy in western India to the second quarter of the nineteenth century. The question of timing is vital. It determines the nature of colonial hegemony in a given region. This hegemony far from being uniform is determined by the outcome of an actual struggle between, among others, dominant classes of the metropolis and indigenous groups. Even when there is collaboration, the terms of collaboration are decided by the strength/weakness of the one in relation to the other. An ongoing struggle settles the matter of strength/weakness. This is an obvious point, but needs to be particularly emphasized when we note the relatively greater capacity for intervention which indigenous groups in Bombay possessed. This had an important bearing on the configuration of power and hence control of urban space.

### Table 1
### Value of Cotton and Opium imported into and Tea exported from Canton under the British flag,
### 1824-1833 (in Spanish dollars)

| Season | Cotton (Imports) | Tea (Exports) | Opium (Imports) |
|---|---|---|---|
| 1824 | 5,220,851 | 8,898,575 | 5,450,000 |
| 1825 | 6,227,740 | 9,087,104 | 9,782,500 |
| 1826 | 7,215,332 | 10,443,775 | 9,269,826 |
| 1827 | 5,787,299 | 9,163,052 | 11,243,496 |
| 1828 | 5,603,953 | 8,540,855 | 10,908,852 |
| 1829 | 5,080,100 | 8,236,568 | 13,450,924 |
| 1830 | 5,628,485 | 8,430,983 | 12,222,525 |
| 1831 | 4,931,243 | 8,520,863 | 11,304,018 |
| 1832 | 5,474,825 | 8,813,171 | 12,185,100 |
| 1833 | 6,726,739 | 8,712,701 | 11,618,716 |
| TOTAL | 57,896,567 | 88,847,647 | 107,435,957 |

Compiled from: H.B. Morse, *The Chronicles of the East India Company Trading to China, 1635-1834* (Oxford, 1926), Vols. III and IV.

Bombay presidency was for long unable to generate sufficient resources to support its civil and military establishments and to finance its Gujarat and Malabar investments. In 1789 the supreme government estimated that Rs.56 lakhs would have to be pumped into the presidency, an echo of Cornwallis' lament of 1788 cited above.[40] In the early years of the nineteenth century, Bombay was still chronically deficient. Fort William was not too pleased to learn from the Bombay government in 1801 that the deficit in that 'Presidency for the current year 1801/2 will probably amount to Rupees 90,25,000.'[41]

Lakshmi Subramanian's entire thesis of an 'Anglo-Bania alliance' in western India (Surat primarily) rests on the indispensability of western Indian sarrafs in facilitating the movement of money from Bengal to the west coast of India.[42] The liquidity crisis confronting Bombay presidency was surmounted by recourse to local credit. Discounting Bengal bills of exchange had become a big business for the sarrafs by mid-eighteenth century. Despite growing colonial penetration of the economy, which unfortunately Subramanian underplays, 'implications of local credit intervention became more pronounced and its ramifcations more extensive' in the last two decades of the century.[43]

The issue was not merely one of finding an appropriate mechanism for the transfer of funds to Bombay. Bombay was a liability in a more fundamental sense. Lack of extensive possessions by the British in western India till the second decade of the nineteenth century prevented Bombay from carrying out the sort of plundering operation which the Company had been engaged in within Bengal and Bihar since Plassey (and more so since the grant of diwani), making it difficult for Bombay to 'internally' finance its purchase of goods for consumption and re-export.

To a large extent the weak political presence of the East India Company in western India throughout the eighteenth century was due to, and reinforced by, Maratha power in the region. From 1706, when Gujarat was first invaded by them, the Marathas successfully encroached upon Mughal authority in the suba till by the middle of the century they effectively controlled most of it.[44] Their initial target had been the area around Surat, but after 1724 they enlarged the area of their operations and by 1736 were entrenched in northern Gujarat.[45] The most powerful Maratha warlords in the suba were the Gaikwads, whose onslaughts brought to an end Mughal rule over Gujarat. By 1753 the Mughals had lost their control over the capital, Ahmadabad.[46] With the formidable Marathas stepping in, it was not very easy for the British to take full advantage of the collapse of Mughal power in Gujarat. Moreover, as we have already noted, Surat/Gujarat was not the focus of the Company's commercial activities in the eighteenth century, there having been a shift to the Coromondal and Bengal. Consequently, in the period immediately following 1761, when Maratha prestige had suffered a setback due to the rout at Panipat, British efforts were aimed primarily at consolidation of their post-Plassey gains in Bengal.

The last quarter of the eighteenth century provided the British with an opportunity for acquiring a firm foothold in western India when the death of the peshwa Madhavrao I led to a prolonged struggle over the question of succession.[47] One of the aspirants, Raghunath Rao, courted the British and promised them possession of Bassein and Salsette. The story thence of intrigue, as well of the struggle among the Maratha sardars and of some of the Maratha chiefs against the British, is long and complicated. The upshot of the whole affair was that British possession of Salsette was confirmed in 1782.[48] This acquisition considerably strengthened the position of Bombay.

By the end of the century establishing British supremacy over western India was very much on the agenda. In 1800 Surat, where British authority had been extensive since 1759, formally came under British rule. The third Anglo-Maratha war (1817-

1818) finally destroyed Maratha power in western India. Annexations in the wake of British victory placed almost the entire western portion of what is today the state of Maharashtra under British rule. Besides, Ahmadabad and a few other territories in Gujarat too came under the direct rule of the company.

What needs to be emphasized is that a very large chunk of territory in western India was still not under British rule. There was Portuguese Daman to the north of Bombay and Goa to the south; there were numerous indigenously ruled states in western India; and Sind had not yet been conquered. In other words, despite the eclipse of Maratha power, which fundamentally altered the balance of power in western and central India in favour of the Company, there still remained a large expanse of territory which was outside of direct/indirect British rule in this region. The process of colonial consolidation was thus prolonged. This was one of the factors that made it possible for Indian traders to take temporary advantage of the expanding trade in the opium produce of western and central India. This temporary advantage had, as we shall see, significant implications for the development of Bombay.[49]

## Notes

[1]    Cf. *Maharashtra State Gazetteer, Greater Bombay District*, Vol. I (Bombay, 1986), p. 2; J.G. da Cunha, *The Origin of Bombay* (Bombay, 1900), pp. 23-24.

[2]    Da Cunha, *Origin of Bombay*, p. 23.

[3]    O.H.K. Spate and A.T.A Learmonth, I*ndia and Pakistan: A General and Regional Geography*, third edition (London, 1967), p. 656.

[4]    *Gazetteer of Bombay City and Island*, 3 vols. (Bombay, 1909), Vol. II, pp. 25; 29-30.

[5]    The relevant articles of the treaty are reproduced in J.J.C. Kol, *A General, Statistical and Historical Report on Portuguese India*, Extracted in 1850 from *Official Documents, BGS*, new series, 10 (Bombay, 1855), pp. 347-348.

6   Bombay was given to the East India Company by Charles II in exchange for a loan of £50,000 repayable at 6% interest, and on an annual payment of £10 rent. *Gazetteer of Bombay City and Island*, Vol. II, pp. 51; 57-58.

7   The ghats are pierced by three passes: Tal, Nana and Bor. These make possible communication between the Konkan coast and the Deccan. At the northern end of the ghats, where the river Tapti flows towards the sea, there is another gap, another point of entry.

8   R.N. Hamilton, resident, Indore, to chairman, Great Indian Peninsular Railway Co., 6 March 1847, NAI, Foreign Department (Political), 89/24 April 1847.

9   *The Bombay Times* and *Journal of Commerce*, 10 July 1840.

10   Cf. K.N. Chaudhuri, *The Trading World of Asia and the English East India Company, 1660-1760*, p.49.

11   Jean de Thevenot in S.N. Sen (ed.), *Indian Travels of Thevenot and Careri* (Delhi, 1949), pp. 8-9; *Travels in India by Jean Baptiste Tavernier*, tr. V. Ball, Vol.I (London, 1889), pp.48-50, 68 and 71-2; Durate Barbosa, T*he Book of Durate Barbosa*, tr. M.L. Dames, Vol.I (London, 1918), p.129; Ashin Das Gupta, *Indian Merchants and the Decline of Surat, c.1700-1750* (Wiesbaden, 1979), p. 8; B.G. Gokhale, *Surat in the Seventeenth Century: A Study in Urban History of Pre-Modern India* (Bombay, 1979), pp.73,77,78 and 80; and Irfan Habib, *An Atlas of the Mughal Empire* (Delhi, 1982), pp. 25 and 58.

12   Cf. Habib, *Atlas*, p.58.

13   Gokhale, *Surat in the Seventeenth Century*, p. 82.

14   F. Warden, *Report on the Landed Tenures of Bombay, 20 August 1814*, BGS, new series, 64 (Bombay, 1861), p. 24.

15   John Burnell, *Bombay in the Days of Queen Anne*, intro. and notes by S.T. Sheppard (London, 1933), p. 61.

16   Holden Furber, *Bombay Presidency in the Mid-Eighteenth Century* (Bombay, 1965), p. 2.

17   *Gujarat State Gazetteers, Surat District*, revised edition (Ahmedabad, 1962), p.14.

18   Referring to the loot of Surat by Shivaji in 1670, in which according to an official enquiry 'Shivaji carried off 66 lakhs of Rupees' worth of booty from Surat', Jadunath Sarkar observes: 'But the real loss of Surat was not to be estimated by the booty which the Marathas carried off. The trade of this,

the richest port of India, was practically destroyed. For several years after Shivaji's withdrawal from it, the town used to throb with panic now and then, whenever any Maratha force came within a few days march of it, or even at false alarms of their coming. ... Business was effectually scared away from Surat, and inland producers hesitated to send their goods to this the greatest emporium of western India'. Jadunath Sarkar, *Shivaji and His Times* (New Delhi, 1973), p. 174.

[19] Das Gupta, *Decline of Surat*, p. 8.

[20] Cf. Gokhale, *Surat in the Seventeenth Century*, p.73.

[21] The answer to this question is not necessarily easy or obvious. If, for instance, we regard the decline of Surat, in the words of David Hardiman, as being "bound up with the increasing penetration and control of India's external trade by European powers in the period after 1500", it might be possible to see the rise of Bombay as a triumph for British enterprise along the west coast. David Hardiman, 'Elite Conflicts in a Trading Empire', Review of Das Gupta, *Indian Merchants and the Decline of Surat*, *EPW*, Vol. XVI, 50 (1981), p.2039.

In the case of Surat one is not entirely convinced that European penetration had indeed become decisive in the early eighteenth century. Das Gupta in a rejoinder has provided evidence indicating that in this period 'European companies at Surat carried no more than one-eighth of the city's maritime commerce'. Ashin Das Gupta, 'Indian Merchants in the Age of Partnership, 1500-1800', Dwijendra Tripathi (ed.), *Business Communities of India: A Historical Perspective* (New Delhi, 1984), p.30.

It does appear that Gujarati commerce, especially with west Asia, was able to withstand the European onslaught till the beginning of the eighteenth century. Gujarati resilience has to be seen in terms of the strong presence of the Ottoman, Safavid and Mughal empires, the crisis at Surat beginning with the decline of these three empires around the turn of the eighteenth century.

[22] Tapan Raychaudhuri and Irfan Habib (eds.), *The Cambridge Economic History of India*, Vol.I (Cambridge, 1982), p.402.

[23] Holden Furber, *Rival Empires of Trade in the Orient, 1600-1800* (Minneapolis, 1976), pp.131-2 and 134.

[24] Chaudhuri, *Trading World of Asia*, p.98.

[25] Holden Furber, *John Company At Work* (Harvard, 1951), p.161.

[26]   Ibid., p.162.

[27]   P.J. Marshall, *East Indian Fortunes: The British in Bengal in the Eighteenth Century* (Oxford, 1976), p.104.

[28]   Ibid.; Furber, *Rival Empires of Trade*, p.131; Chaudhuri, *Trading World of Asia*, p.98; Ashin Das Gupta, 'India and the Indian Ocean in the Eighteenth Century', in Ashin Das Gupta and M.N. Pearson (eds), *India and the Indian Ocean: 1500-1800* (Calcutta, 1987), p.143.

[29]   In his earlier *John Company at Work* (p.164) and in his later *Rival Empires of Trade* (p.279), published in the same year as Marshall's *East Indian Fortunes*.

[30]   Marshall, *East Indian Fortunes*, p.104.

[31]   Ibid.

[32]   Cornwallis to Henry Dundas, 4 November 1788, Charles Ross (ed.), *Correspondence of Charles, First Marquis Cornwallis*, Vol.I, second edition (London, 1859), p.390.

[33]   Ibid.

[34]   Cornwallis to Dundas, 4 November 1788, *Correspondence of Cornwallis*, Vol. I, p.390.

[35]   Cornwallis to William Pitt, 6 November 1788, ibid., p.391.

[36]   Ibid.

[37]   Pamela Nightingale, *Trade and Empire in Western India, 1784-1806* (Cambridge, 1970), p.23.

[38]   Ibid.

[39]   Trade between China and England with tea as the main commodity had been rapidly expanding right from the beginning of the eighteenth century. The Commutation Act of 1784 only gave further encouragement to it. K.N. Chaudhuri notes that the first decade of the eighteenth century 'was the critical decade of take-off for tea consumption on a large scale'. Chaudhuri, *Trading World of Asia*, p.388.

[40]   See Lakshmi Subramanian, 'Banias and the British: The Role of Indigenous Credit in the Process of Imperial Expansion in Western India, in the Second Half of the Eighteenth Century', *MAS*, Vol. XXI, 3 (1987), p.485.

[41]   Fort William to Bombay Govt., 23 July 1801, NAI, HD, Misc. Letters.

[42] Subramanian, 'Banias and the British', pp.473-510.

[43] Ibid., p.493. M. Torri in a critique of Subramanian contends that the traditional sarraf network at Surat was on the verge of collapse towards the end of the eighteenth century 'largely because of political and economic changes brought about by the rising colonial order'. M. Torri, 'Trapped inside the Colonial Order: The Hindu Bankers of Surat and their Business World during the Second Half of the Eighteenth Century', *MAS*, Vol.XV, 2 (1991), p.369.

[44] M.S. Commissariat, *A History of Gujarat*, Vol. II (Bombay, 1957), p.453.

[45] Ibid.

[46] Ibid., pp.511-514. The final capture of Ahmadabad in 1758 eventually marked the end of Mughal rule in Gujarat. Ibid., p.533.

[47] G.S. Sardesai, *New History of the Marathas*, Vol. III (Bombay, 1948), pp.11 ff.

[48] Ibid., p.118.

[49] Amiya Bagchi has pointed out that the stronger position of Indian merchants in Bombay during the early nineteenth century, as compared to Calcutta and Madras, had its roots in 'the continued resistance of Indian rulers against British conquest ... and the survival, in however a truncated form, of a large number of native states in that part of the country, which provided a base of operations and a sanctuary for Indian traders and financiers'. Moreover, 'the fact that cotton and opium were both cultivated by unregulated peasants rather than under company monopoly and were valuable commodities in the China trade also played an important role'. Amiya K. Bagchi, 'Transition to British Indian Systems of Money and Banking, 1800-1850', *MAS*, Vol. XIX, 3 (1985), p.511.

# BOMBAY AND THE TRADE
# IN MALWA OPIUM

Overwhelmed by nostalgia for the colonial era some popular works on Bombay revel in selective images of the city, choosing such landmarks and such moments in its history as might conjure pleasant memories for those who look back on the days of the British raj with longing.[1] While there might not apparently be much harm in isolated nostalgic evocations, one has to guard against the distortions that could be, and often are, introduced by allowing a desire for some aesthetically more appealing experiences of that era to become desire for the days of the raj. Further, one must be careful that the ugly is not easily ignored. As much as one might like to suggest that learning to play cricket and thinking 'more or less in the European manner', gave indigenous groups the wherewithal to participate in the economic development of Bombay and that social intercourse with the British was responsible for the success story of Bombay,[2] the fact remains that the destiny of Bombay as a great commercial and industrial centre was born of its becoming an accomplice in the drugging of countless Chinese with opium, a venture in which the Indian business class showed great zeal alongside the East India Company. This is the sordid underside of Bombay's colonial past.

The story of the formation of the Indian capitalist class in Bombay is a story both of collaboration and conflict. The feature of economic activity in western and central India which illustrates, most vividly, the vigour of Indian enterprise in the region during the early nineteenth century is trade in opium. In the case of Bombay the significance of trade in this commodity derives from the capacity of Indian merchants to thwart attempts of the British Indian government to establish a monopoly of the Bengal type over opium in western and central India. They were encouraged in their truculence by the tacit or active support of numerous other indigenous groups ranging from Indian rulers in the region, with their curtailed authority, to armed bandits. The divergent policies pursued with regard to the opium produce of the Ganga region ('Bengal' opium), on the one hand, and that of Malwa and Rajasthan (Malwa opium), on the other, must be kept in view in the context of far-reaching implications which a non-monopolistic policy, forced on the British in western India, had on the development of Bombay.

Modern Bombay, in a sense, has its genesis in poppy fields of Bihar. Large-scale exports of Indian opium to south-east Asia commenced in the seventeenth century when the drug became one of the commodities in the Dutch East India Company's intra-Asian trade. There were two major opium producing areas in India: the Ganga region, where initially Bihar was the main supplier, and Malwa. The Dutch procured most of their opium from Bihar. By the mid-seventeenth century Bihar opium was the principal commodity being carried by the Dutch company (VOC) from Bengal to the Indonesian archipelago. According to Om

Prakash 'the quantity exported had reached fairly important levels' towards the end of the 1660s.[3] Employees of the VOC also privately exported substantial quantities of Bihar opium to ports such as Batavia, though they were officially prohibited from trading on their own account.[4] There was almost an eight-fold increase in the profits earned by the VOC from the sale of Bihar opium in Indonesian markets between the late 1670s and the 1740s.[5] In 1745 the Dutch company set up the Opium Society so as to allow private traders to participate in the opium trade on a limited basis while ensuring overall control of the VOC.[6] Private traders were already so numerous that the Opium Society was not entirely successful in regulating the commerce. In any case the VOC soon lost access to supplies of Bihar opium after the conquest of Bengal and Bihar by the English East India Company. They virtually withdrew from the trade during the latter half of the century.

From the early 1760s servants of the English East India Company in their private capacity, and eventually the Company itself, tried to corner the entire supply of Bihar opium. To start with, the head of the Company's factory in Patna attempted to personally monopolize the opium produce of the region for the purpose of export. Then in 1765 Company officials launched a joint venture to collectively trade in the drug.[7] The size of profits from the trade was too large for it to be left in the hands of individuals, and 1773 Warren Hastings abolished free trade in it.[8] Henceforth the Company had an exclusive right to all the opium produced in its territories in eastern India. When Banaras and the area around it were placed directly under the Company's administration in 1795 the opium monopoly was extended to Banaras-Ghazipur. This was another prime opium-producing tract. Opium from Banaras-Ghazipur and Bihar, officially referred to as 'Benaras opium' and 'Patna opium' respectively, was marketed under the brand name 'Bengal opium'.

In 1797 the Company modified its earlier policy of purchasing opium through contractors and began procuring the entire produce directly. A comprehensive regulation of 1799 (Bengal Regulation VI) brought the cultivation of opium under the complete control of the Company.[9] The cultivation of the poppy crop and extraction of raw opium from it was left to peasant producers. The peasants had to obtain a license from the Company that specified the actual area on which the crop was to be grown. The entire produce was supposed to be handed over to the Company's officials. Raw opium was processed and packed by the Company in its own establishments so that it was partly involved in production as well. All this opium was taken to Calcutta (some of the more inferior produce having been reserved for 'internal' consumption) where it was auctioned exclusively for export. The bulk of the opium purchased at Calcutta went to China. As Chinese imperial authorities had banned the import of the drug into the country, the Company found it more convenient to realize profits through these auctions and then leave it to private traders to take the risk of carrying the contraband cargoes and smuggling them into China.

The East India Company had barely settled down to enjoy the fruits of its Bengal monopoly when disturbing reports began flowing in about the export of opium from the west coast. One report suggested that perhaps more than a thousand chests (a chest may be taken as containing 140 lbs of the drug) had been exported from Bombay alone between 1800 and 1803.[10] Opium was also making its way to China from other ports such as Goa and Surat.[11] It was only then that the Company learnt for the first time that opium produced in the Malwa region had the potential of becoming a serious rival to Bengal opium in the China market. The obvious response was a complete ban, in 1805, on the export of opium through Bombay. Simultaneously the Indian states in Gujarat and some other parts of western India were asked to restrict the production of the drug in their respective territories and block its passage to the coast.[12] The company's objective at this stage was the 'ultimate annihilation' of Malwa opium.[13]

Malwa[14] was well-known for its opium at least since the sixteenth century.[15] It would appear that the opium sold as 'Cambay opium' at markets along the west coast in the sixteenth and seventeenth centuries was in fact the produce of Malwa.[16] The massive expansion of opium exports from Bengal to China in the closing decades of the nineteenth century drew Indo-Portuguese and Indian traders to this alternative source of supply.[17] The long association of Indo-Portuguese traders with the sea-borne commerce of the west coast, combined with the links that they had with the Portuguese at Macao who actively participated in the smuggling of the drug into China, gave them a distinct advantage. It is no coincidence that large exports of the drug from India's west coast were more or less pioneered by Roger de Faria, an Indo-Portuguese trader from Goa.

Roger (Rogério) de Faria was born in Goa in 1770.[18] His father, João de Faria, was connected with the China trade. João went to China for a short while (in all likelihood to Macao) and on his return became a partner in the firm Bruce, Faria and Co. at Calcutta.[19] Roger de Faria too was initially based in Calcutta. In his mid-twenties he was undertaking regular voyages to Macao. We have a reference to a visit he made to Macao in December 1798.[20] Even before that, c. 1796, he had been granted permission to trade at Macao, a privilege allowed at this time only to the Portuguese.[21] De Faria eventually settled down in Bombay sometime after 1800.[22] He maintained close links with firms in Goa, especialy V. Nariana Camotim (Kamat).[23]

De Faria was part of a group of Indo-Portuguese traders who procured Malwa opium from Bombay, Daman and Surat for onward shipment to Macao (though not necessarily as partners). These traders had set up their base at Bombay rather than at Goa since the capital of the Portuguese Estado da Índia was situated at too great a distance from the main Malwa supply networks. Bombay was their preferred port due the facilities for export that were becoming available there. Further, just a stone's throw away from Bombay was the Portuguese enclave of Daman which was to play a crucial role in keeping the trade in Malwa opium alive following the restrictions that the East India Company imposed in 1805. Between 1805 and 1821 Daman was the main outlet for Malwa opium. However the big opium dealers conducted the trade from Bombay. In the long run most of the benefits accrued to Bombay rather than to Daman.

Apart from de Faria there were two other prominent Indo-Portuguese merchants who were active in the Malwa opium export trade at the beginning of the century: Jose Francisco Pereira and Maj. António Pereira. J.F. Pereira's firm, Pereira and Co., had extensive dealings in opium at Bombay during the first quarter of the nineteenth century. His involvement with opium began around the turn of the century. In 1805 a consignment of 254 chests of opium was transported by Jose Pereira from Daman to Goa, to be taken to Macao.[24] The Company's ban meant that Bombay had to be avoided. Jose Pereira had strong ties with the Camotim firm at Goa.[25] His associate in Daman was Daya Ram Dulobha who was one of the leading opium dealers at that port.[26] Pereira was the owner of a 300-ton ship, the *Angelica*, which regularly carried the drug to Macao.[27] Similarly António Pereira bought opium at Daman and had it shipped directly to Macao or else via Goa. An 1815 report of the British envoy to Goa referred to several trips made by António Pereira from Goa to Daman to carry on his opium business. On one occasion the Portuguese viceroy provided a brig of war to escort a consignment of Pereira's opium from Goa to Macao.[28] António Pereira had access to the Company's officials in Bombay as well. Among other things, he was related to the leading Bombay trader Miguel de Lima e Souza who enjoyed the confidence of the Bombay government.[29]

We find de Faria shuttling between Bombay, Daman and Goa to contract for opium cargoes and ship these to Macao. He owned one ship at this stage, the *Grã Cruz de Aviz*.[30] In 1816 he was busy loading an opium consignment on the ship *Leal Português*, bound for Macao. In 1817 he was preparing a consignment for the *Angelica*.[31] Macao records show that the ship arrived at that port laden with opium.[32] De Faria's correspondence indicates that some of the opium on the *Angelica* belonged to António Pereira.[33] As de Faria's business became more prosperous he had a ship built for himself at Daman in 1817. This was the *Glorioso*, a 490-ton vessel, that figures frequently in records relating to opium.[34] De Faria subsequently acquired two more ships: *Boa Esperança* and *Margaret Crawford*.[35] The *Glorioso* was later rechristened *Dom Manoel de Portugal*. He set up the firm of Sir Roger de Faria and Co. in Bombay with Luis Francisco da Silva, Francisco António da Carvalho (his brother-in-law) and Jose Maria Pinto as his junior partners.[36] The business of the firm extended to Brazil, Mozambique and Portugal.[37] Nevertheless opium remained the mainstay of de Faria's trading empire.

It is this group of Indo-Portuguese traders that at an early stage undermined the Company's efforts to restrict exports of Malwa opium. This was a difficult time for the Portuguese settlements on the west coast as they were under British military occupation/protection for several years due to the Napoleonic Wars. Yet it was precisely in this period that the trade acquired such proportions as would render it impossible for the Company to stamp out Malwa opium exports. D.E. Owen has noted that it was by 1818 that the competition between the Bengal and Malwa varieties had 'become critical' in China.[38]

The third Anglo-Maratha war, soon after the end of the Napoleonic Wars, established British supremacy in western India. In the post-1818 period the Company first tried to enforce the ban on Malwa opium exports more vigorously,[39] but soon had to acknowledge that the trade was too voluminous to be suppressed altogether. It therefore decided to buy up supplies of Malwa opium and auction the drug for export as was done in the case of Bengal opium. There was, of course, one really crucial difference. The Company had no control over production and had to get its supplies from the open market. Malwa opium was auctioned at Bombay and Calcutta from the 1821 season.[40] A large proportion of the produce of Malwa continued to be sold at Daman. There were thus two varieties of Malwa opium in the market: Company Malwa and Daman Malwa. The Company's Malwa opium had to compete with Daman Malwa, while Bengal opium had to compete with both. As for the Bombay merchants they had the option of buying opium at Daman if the prices at the auctions were too high. It may be mentioned in passing that Bombay merchants did not confine themselves to Malwa opium but additionally invested in Bengal opium.

In 1823-24 the Company modified its Malwa opium policy. It was no longer willing to buy the drug in the wholesale markets of Malwa. Instead it exerted political pressure on the Indian-ruled states (Malwa opium was grown entirely in states that were under 'indirect rule') to supply specified quantities of opium to the Company at fixed prices and to limit the cultivation of poppy in their respective territories. The experiment with this policy lasted till the end of the twenties when the Company gave up its direct participation in the trade.[41]

By the 1820s a large number of Parsis, Marwaris, Gujarati Banias and Konkani Muslims had moved into the opium trade at Bombay. There is an impression that the Parsis completely dominated the trade.[42] The names that we have of indigenous firms/merchants dealing with opium at Bombay, c. 1803-1830, show that out of 120 firms/merchants (excluding European, Armenian and Indo-Portuguese dealers) that are alluded to in official records, just 49 were Parsi. Of these, three were partnerships with non-Parsis (though there might have been more). In other words Parsis accounted for just a little over one-third of the firms/merchants.[43] They still were a numerically large group and their share of the trade was sizeable. As a business community the Parsis of Bombay were among the first Indians to develop commercial links with China during the colonial period. The brothers Hirji and Muncherji Readymoney are supposed to have inaugurated the Parsi connection with China in the latter half of the eighteenth century.[44]

It needs to be underlined that the opium commerce of Bombay was not an exclusive Parsi preserve. The big players were Remington Crawford and Co., Jamsetjee Jejeebhoy, Motichund Amichund (and later his son Khemchund), Hormasji Dorabji, Nagardass Hirji Mody, Madowdass Ransordass, Mohammad Ali Rogay, Roger de Faria, and on a somewhat smaller scale Cursetji Ardaseer and Aga Mohammad Suastry. A large number of traders, brokers, financiers and shipowners too had their investments in opium, though this may not have been their primary business.

Of these we may mention Framji Cowasji Banaji, Cursetji Cowasji, Pestonji Bomanji Wadia, Hormasji Bomanji Wadia, Juggonath Sunkersett, Dhakji Dadaji and Viccaji Merji.

For about two decades, from the mid-1820s to the mid-1840s, the figure who dominated the opium trade at Bombay was Jamsetjee Jejeebhoy (1783-1859). He was the first Indian to be knighted (1842) and the first to receive a baronetcy (1857). These honours have ensured that the details of his life are well-known. Yet, many aspects of his early career are quite obscure. What we know is that he was born in Bombay, where his family resided in the Fort area, that when still a small child he returned with his parents to Navasari from where they had originally come, and came back to Bombay in 1799 as an assistant in the shop of his maternal uncle Framji Nusserwanji Battliwala.[45] Battliwala dealt in empty bottles but seems to have turned to the China trade.[46]

Small businessmen with a little money to spare were tempted to invest in opium and cotton at the port. Newspapers regularly published notices announcing the departure of ships for China and inviting custom. A typical advertisement which appeared in the weekly *Bombay Courier*—many of the notices were in Gujarati—in 1800, stated that the ship *Mansoory* would 'positively' be sailing soon and asked readers to apply to Aga Mohammad 'merchant of Bombay' for particulars.[47] Aga Mohammad later emerged as one of the prominent opium traders of Bombay. His premises were located inside the Fort next door to that of the merchant Ramdass Manordass.[48] The shops of petty traders like Battliwala (we are not very certain about the scale of his empty bottle business) were situated cheek by jowl with the offices of the shipping agents and opium speculators in the Fort area. Not much effort was needed to get involved in small-scale opium speculations. Moreover, it was common for young Parsi men to sail to China to try their luck there. One should bear in mind that several ships owned by Parsis plied regularly between Bombay and China. The formative phase of Jamsetjee's career fits into this pattern. He undertook four voyages to China between 1800 and 1808.[49]

Jamsetjee's first trip to China was as *mehta* (accounts clerk) of his cousin Merwanji Manockji Tabak.[50] In a reversal of fortunes Merwanji was later employed by Jamsetjee as his principal agent in China where Merwanji was stationed for several years till his death in 1830.[51] Jamsetjee' second voyage was as a partner in the firm of Battliwala.[52] On his fourth and last voyage Jamsetjee was taken prisoner on his return journey when the ship on which he was travelling, the *Brunswick*, was captured by the French. After several adventures Jamsetjee returned to Bombay in 1807-08.[53] Siddiqi has brought to light a vital piece of information regarding Jamsetjee's journey aboard the *Brunswick*. It was 'on the *Brunswick*, Jamsetjee made the acquaintance of the ship's assistant surgeon, the young William Jardine'.[54] This meeting marked the inception of a long business relationship. While Jardine went on to create, alongwith James Matheson, the largest opium trading network in China, Jamsetjee emerged as their main supplier at Bombay. All these were, however, developments of the twenties.

It is unlikely that Jamsetjee would have had much capital at his disposal at this stage. He had suffered major financial losses in the Great Fire of 1803 (which we will discuss in more detail in the next essay)[55] and then there was the setback of his fourth China voyage. The change in his fortunes between c. 1810-1820 might have had something to do with his association with Roger de Faria. When that association commenced we do not know, but Jamsetjee did a stint as a clerk (*escrevente*) in de Faria's establishment.[56] Jamsetjee had in the meantime married

Battliwala's daughter and the partnership with his father-in-law lasted till Battliwala's death in 1818.[57] By now Jamsetjee was sufficiently affluent and had even bought a ship of his own in 1814, the *Good Success*.[58] In the ten years or so between 1814 and 1823 Jamsetjee came to be recognized as one of the principal merchants of Bombay. His name does not yet figure in the list of leading 'European and Native mercantile establishments' whose sentiments were sought in 1817 by a committee set up by the government to revise the customs regulations of Bombay Presidency. Besides the European establishments (Remington Crawford and Co., Forbes and Co., Shotton and Co., and Leckie and Co. appear at the top of the list) the committee requested Roger de Faria, Hormasji Bomanji (Wadia), Framji Cowasji (Banaji) and Ramdass Manordas (referred to above) for their opinion on the subject.[59] Neither was Jamsetjee yet part of the small circle of opium magnates who are mentioned together in a power of attorney document executed in favour of Roger de Faria and Co. in 1818. The signatories include Motichund Amichund, Mohammad Ali Rogay, Merwanji Hirji and Jehangir Cowasji Patel.[60]

Among the earliest public documents in which Jamsetjee Jejeebhoy finds mention is a petition of 1820 from 'merchants and other native inhabitants engaged in Commercial Pursuits at the Presidency of Bombay' addressed to the governor, Mountstuart Elphinstone. The petition relates to customs duties and requests the government to lower certain duties and abolish some other. Jamsetjee's name is at the head of sixty-three signatories.[61] His opium business was now thriving. The letterbooks of James Matheson, which begin in 1820, refer to the arrival in mid-1821 of a consignment of 339 chests of Malwa opium, of which 289 were consigned to Merwanji Manockji.[62] Although he is not referred to as Jamsetjee's agent in China in this instance, the later correspondence does make it clear that Merwanji was working for Jamsetjee.[63] The special relationship between Jamsetjee on the one hand and Jardine Matheson and Co. and its predecessor companies on the other came into being around the middle of the decade. From the 1820s a considerable volume of all the Malwa opium consigned to China from Bombay and Daman passed through the hands of these companies.

Charles Magniac, one of the predecessor companies of Jardine Matheson and Co. (Jardine Matheson and Co. was established by William Jardine and James Matheson in 1832), did not as yet in the early 1820s rely on Jamsetjee's consignments of Malwa opium to the extent that it came to in the latter half of the decade.[64] At the Indian end Magniac had connections with, among others, Roger de Faria. Much interest was shown in the opium that de Faria was engaged in loading aboard the *Angelica*, then at Goa, in March 1821.[65] In January 1825 de Faria was writing to Charles Magniac that his firm had admitted Jose Maria Pinto as a partner in August 1824. The letter suggests that de Faria had been constantly dealing with Magniac.[66] The link survived down to the 1830s. Another Bombay merchant who was regularly consigning his opium to Charles Magniac since the beginning of the decade was Hormasji Dorabji. Hormasji had sent out an agent, Framji Muncherji, to China to look after his interests.[67] From 1824-25 onwards the relationship between Jamsetjee and Magniac was not merely that of a merchant consigning goods to an agent, but one that at a deeper level involved mutual cooperation and promoting each others' business.

While Magniac and Co. tried to corner as large a share of the opium supplies flowing into China, Jamsetjee and his associates attempted to do the same in Bombay and Daman.

Jamsetjee's main associates were Motichund Amichund, Mohammad Ali Rogay, Hormasji Dorabji and Roger de Faria. All of them were consigning their opium, not exclusively though, to Magniac and Co. Jamsetjee, Motichund and Mohammad Ali were partners in a firm that lasted till the early thirties.[68] Afterwards they carried on their business separately. Hormasji and de Faria had their own establishments. We can see the big five combining to keep out smaller dealers and using each others' ships (or chartering vessels from other friends) to transport Malwa opium to China. Hormasji as well as de Faria had extensive contacts in Daman and their role was crucial for procuring Daman Malwa. Hormasji is a forgotten figure as his business declined following severe losses that he sustained in 1832.[69] One of the partners of Hormasji was the important opium dealer Nagardass Hirji Mody.[70]

As we have already noted, from 1824 the Company mounted pressure on the indigenously ruled states of western India to check trade in Malwa opium, and sell specified quantities of the opium produced in their respective territories exclusively to the Company. It also kept a strict vigil at ports to prevent the export of the drug. None of these measures succeeded in giving to the Company access to the entire exportable produce of Malwa opium. Large quantities remained within an indigenously controlled network. The Scindia state, the single largest producer of opium in the region, did not accept the restrictive measures that the Company had proposed though negotiations with the Scindia darbar dragged on till the end of the decade. The Company's strategy could scarcely have been effective without the inclusion of the Scindia state.[71] Most of the states which had agreed to implement the Company's Malwa policy had done so reluctantly and powerful opium lobbies in these states often had the backing of the rulers themselves in their endeavours to bypass the restrictive measures.[72]

Indian traders demonstrated great ingenuity and resourcefulness in perfecting an alternative route for the passage of opium from Malwa to the west coast. The route completely avoided British-administered territories. The main route was from northern Malwa to Pali in Rajasthan; from Pali via Jaisalmer to Karachi; from Karachi by sea to Daman. The period from 1824 to 1831 was the golden era of the Daman opium market. Daman prices were a reference point for the prices quoted at the Bombay auctions. There were of course several variables that had to be taken into account while determining opium prices in general – prices and the demand in China; the production in Malwa; prices quoted at the Calcutta auctions; and the quantity that was available at Daman. What is significant is that so long as the Daman route was thriving Bombay opium exporters were not dependent upon the Company alone for their supplies. And they worked hard to reduce even this dependence by promoting the Daman trade.

We have details of one set of Daman consignments and can get from these an idea about how the system operated and the linkages and personal relationships that sustained it. In April 1825 Motichund Amichund was planning to purchase some opium from the Daman market for shipment to China. He contracted with J. Augustinho da Silva, owner of the brig *Caçador*, to sail from Bombay to Daman to load '250 to 300' chests of opium. A.G. Frith was named the captain of the ship. The freight charges were Spanish$10 per chest. The amount was payable sixty days after the safe arrival of the ship in China. Da Silva's vessel was to proceed to Macao. The government duties and boat hire at Macao were to be paid by Motichund's agent there. If necessary the agent or the consignee could direct the ship to go to Lintin.[73] According to the contract 'should my [Motichund's] agent in China wish to employ the Brig Caçador as a godown at Lintin, Mr Frith shall proceed there, and stay with the aforesaid quantity till the latter end of November next ensuing, with an additional Freight of 2 dollars per chest per month'.[74] Each consignment always involved considerable risk and one had to wait for several months for the returns, if any. This was after all a smuggling enterprise.

In the first week of May Jamsetjee wrote to Charles Magniac informing them that Motichund Amichund had shipped 229 chests of opium aboard the *Caçador*. The opium was consigned to Magniac. He added, 'We also prevailed on him, that in conjunction with his other friends he should make further shipments per the Portuguese ship Angelica also to your consignment in an increased quantity, and are glad to learn that the latter shipment had already commenced at Demaun...'.[75] Jamsetjee was thus obliging Magniac, Jose Pereira (owner of *Angelica* and an old friend of de Faria), and Motichund. The *Angelica* carried 224 chests of opium belonging to Motichund, 'said by those who examined and packed it, to be of the very best quality'.[76] Some of Motichund's 'friends' might also have invested in this opium.

In prompting Motichund, Jamsetjee was simultaneously obliging Remington Crawford and Co. and Jardine while Motichund was reinforcing his links with them. Jardine was in Bombay at this time. He had agreed to advance Rs.1 lakh on these consignments, at three-quarters per cent per month interest. Remington Crawford too had advanced some money to Moti-chund for the same purpose. Further, the consignments were insured by Remington Crawford.[77] Jardine for his part was using his contacts in Bombay, who included Jamsetjee, to get more opium exporters to consign their opium to his firm and even offered them incentives in the form of advances. He made it a point to request Magniac to 'realize such prices, as will induce the parties to repeat the consignments in seasons to come'.[78]

One can discern four kinds of opium transactions at Bombay (see Appendix A). There were firstly the big purchasers at the Bombay auctions. They bought some of this opium on their own account to be consigned to agents in China. As we have seen, Malwa opium was increasingly consigned to Magniac/Jardine Matheson. Some of it, though on a much smaller scale, was also sent to Indian agents in Canton. Another agency house to which opium was consigned in China was Dent and Co. Siddiqi has argued that given the constraints under which the Indian merchants operated due to colonial domination, the consignment trade actually subsidized the agency houses: 'The consignment trade, simply because the shipper bore the entire risk, in effect provided the agency houses both with working capital free of interest, and with stocks, the property of the shippers, which they could sell as they pleased. The consequences for the shippers were doubly disadvantageous. They bore the brunt of price fluctuations and, as Jamsetjee and his clients discovered, of manipulation on the part of their agents in the accounting of sales'.[79] The big dealers bought some of the opium at the auctions on behalf of the Portuguese merchants in Macao and agency houses in China.

Second, there were the petty traders at auctions who usually bought the opium for on-the-spot sale to actual exporters.[80] Price fluctuations from one auction to the next in a season and even during the course of a particular auction attracted small-scale investors looking for quick returns. The smaller buyers sometimes held back their stocks in the hope of realizing a better profit. The uncertainties inherent in this trade made it a gambling venture for almost everyone. For the petty speculators the element of chance was often greater as they lacked the kind of information that the bulk dealers had access to.

Third, there were the purchases made by Bombay merchants, again both big and small, at Daman. Bombay and Daman virtually constituted a unified market in this period for the purpose of Malwa opium. The physical proximity of the two ports facilitated their interlinking. There was one major difference here. Unlike at the Company's auctions, where at least the dealers had a rough idea right at the beginning of the season as to the number of chests that would be put up for auction, it was virtually impossible to estimate the quantity of opium that would arrive in the Daman market. This made it difficult to judge the appropriate price to be paid for the drug. An additional problem was that the quality of the opium at Daman was never uniform as it was procured from diverse sources and passed through several hands. The big dealers were extremely careful about assessing the quality of the opium they bought at Daman. No wonder Jardine specially mentioned that Motichund's 1825 consignment referred to above was 'of the very best quality'. The smaller dealers from Bombay would have had to be a little wary, the more so if they were not very familiar with the business. Finally, there was the opium purchased by Bombay merchants at the Calcutta auctions. This was something that only the bigger merchants could afford to do.

Indigenous shipping and the opium trade were closely interlinked at Bombay. The west coast had a dynamic tradition of shipbuilding during the early colonial period. The major shipbuilding docks in the eighteenth century were Surat, Daman, Bombay, Mazagaon and Cochin. The association of the Parsis with the shipbuilding industry of Bombay is well documented.[81]

Konkani Muslims had a strong presence in coastal shipping.[82] Most of the leading opium merchants had their own ships. Conversely, most of the big shipowners had investments in opium. The brothers Pestonji Bomanji (1758-1816) and Hormasji Bomanji (1766-1826), belonging to the famous Wadia family of master shipbuilder fame, owned several ships. Hormasji, and perhaps Pestonji, invested some of their money in opium. Pestonji's adopted son Dadabhoy Pestonji (1802-1885) and Hormasji's son Bomanji Hormasji (1808-1862) retained their interests in shipping while dealing in opium on a large scale. The Wadias diversified into real estate and banking.[83] Jamsetjee initially made his fortune through opium and invested part of this in shipping. Following is a list of some of the ships owned by opium traders of Bombay (other than the ships of de Faria and Jose Pereira that we have already mentioned). The majority of these ships were familiar names in the opium business right from Gujarat to China. This is not a comprehensive list. Not all ships carrying opium, as for instance most Portuguese ships, were registered at Bombay and some of the vessels kept changing hands. At times the real owner could be different from the registered owner. There might also be multiple shares in a ship.

By 1829 the East India Company had come to the conclusion that it was no longer possible to continue with the Malwa opium policy that it had been pursuing since 1823.[84] Rampant smuggling showed no signs of abating (Table 3). Arrivals at Daman outstripped the quantities procured by the Company and had an adverse impact on Bombay prices. The Company had a stock of 3600 chests for the 1830 auctions whereas it was estimated that nearly 10,000 chests would reach Daman.[85] At this stage the Bombay government suggested that if this opium could be brought to Bombay on the payment of a duty the Company could then at

## Table 2

### Ships owned by prominent opium dealers of Bombay, c. early 19th century

| Name of Ship | Tons | Built at | Year |
|---|---|---|---|
| (JAMSETJEE JEJEEBHOY) | | | |
| 1. Bombay Castle | 602 | Cochin | 1816 |
| 2. Fort William | 1214 | Calcutta | 1803 |
| 3. Good Success | 545 | Daman | 1817 |
| 4. Charlotte | 691 | Bombay | 1802 |
| 5. Shaw Kusroo | 190 | Daman | —— |
| 6. Shah Byramgore | 525 | Calcutta | 1800 |
| 7. Johnny | 79 | Manila | 1813 |
| | | | |
| (MOTICHUND AMICHUND AND KHEMCHUND MOTICHUND) | | | |
| 1. Bombay | 602 | Mazagaon | 1835 |
| 2. Clairmont | 328 | Bombay | 826 |
| 3. Lady Grant | 239 | Mazagaon | 1835 |
| 4. Cornwallis | 666 | Surat | 1788 |
| 5. Hannah | 457 | Bombay | 1811 |
| 6. Conde de Rio Pardo | 430 | Daman | 1817 |
| | | | |
| (FRAMJI COWASJI) | | | |
| 1. Golconda | 858 | —— | —— |
| 2. Sullemany | 679 | Daman | 1799 |
| 3. Buckinghamshire | 1731 | Bombay | 1816 |

**(CURSETJI COWASJI)**

| | | | |
|---|---|---|---|
| 1. Ardaseer | 422 | Bombay | 1836 |
| 2. Castle Huntley | 1300 | Calcutta | 1812 |
| 3. Charles Grant | 1253 | Bombay | 1826 |
| 4. Pearl | —— | Bombay | 1837 |

**(AGA MOHAMMAD)**

| | | | |
|---|---|---|---|
| 1. Discovery | 289 | —— | —— |
| 2. Sir Robert Compton | 346 | Bombay | 1835 |
| 3. Clairmont | 328 | Bombay | 1826 |
| 4. Travancore | 477 | Cochin | —— |
| 5. Hariett | —— | Bengal | —— |

**(CURSETJI ARDASEER)**

| | | | |
|---|---|---|---|
| 1. Pascoa | 802 | Calcutta | —— |
| 2. Scaleby Castle | 1242 | Bombay | 1798 |

**(PESTONJI BOMANJI/HORMASJI BOMANJI)**

| | | | |
|---|---|---|---|
| 1. Anne | 788 | Bombay | 1812 |
| 2. Milford | 670 | Bombay | 1786 |
| 3. Friendship | 872 | Daman | 1794 |
| 4. Lowjee Family | 925 | Bombay | 1795 |

**(HORMASJI DORABJI)**

| | | | |
|---|---|---|---|
| 1. Lord Castlereagh | 762 | Cochin | 1804 |

**(VICCAJI MERJI)**

| | | | |
|---|---|---|---|
| 1. Caledonia | 710 | Bombay | 1824 |

Compiled from: *East India Register; Bombay Calendar and Almanac* least earn a large revenue from it, a whopping Rs.17.5 lakhs per annum on 10,000 chests if the duty was Rs.175 per chest as was initially recommended.[86] This would be in addition to the duty on the chests hitherto brought for auction. A new policy was introduced in 1830 under which any quantity of Malwa opium could be brought freely to Bombay for the purpose of export on the payment of a duty. The restrictions imposed on the Malwa states were removed and the opium treaties were annulled. The auctions were discontinued.

### Table 3
### Exports of Malwa Opium to China,
### from Bombay and Daman (chests)

| Season | Bombay* | Daman |
|--------|---------|-------|
| 1821 | 1600 | 678 |
| 1822 | 1600 | 2255 |
| 1823 | 1500 | 1535 |
| 1824 | 1500 | 2063 |
| 1825 | 2500 | 1563 |
| 1826 | 2500 | 1605 |
| 1827 | 2980 | 1524 |
| 1828 | 3820 | 3889 |
| 1829 | 3502 | 4597 |
| 1830 | 3720 | 9136 |

* Excludes Malwa chests auctioned at Calcutta.
Source: John Phipps, *A Practical Treatise on the China and Eastern Trade ... etc.* (Calcutta, 1835), p. 235.

The new policy became operative from the 1831 season. Opium passes were issued at the rate of Rs.175 per chest till 1835, when the duty was lowered to Rs.125 because of the continuing competition from Daman. In 1834-1835 passes were granted for nearly 7000 chests to be exported via Bombay.[87] During the same season reportedly 5600 chests were exported from Daman.[88] The smuggling route remained active till the end of the 1830s and was eventually abandoned after the First Opium War (1839-1842). The Opium War coincided with another event, namely the conquest of Sind. The annexation of Sind in 1843 blocked the route from Rajasthan to Karachi. A reinterpretation of the evidence on the conquest of Sind suggests that 'some correlation existed between British opium policy on the one hand and the decision to annex Sind'.[89] With the military occupation of Karachi by British troops in 1839, supplies to Daman dried up. The Company was now in a position to increase the duty on Malwa opium. By 1848 it had risen to Rs.400 per chest.[90]

The decline of Daman was hastened by the internal political conflicts at Goa and Daman. In the struggle for power in the Portuguese territories during the mid-1830s, following the promulgation of a liberal constitution in Portugal in 1833, Roger de Faria supported the government of Bernardo Peres da Silva that had been ousted at Goa. Peres da Silva was the first Indo-Portuguese Goan to be appointed to head the government of Portuguese India (1834). He was however forced to flee from the city, and sought shelter in Daman.[91] Here he received the support and financial assistance of de Faria. In return de Faria was to receive certain exemptions on customs duties. This might have been a desperate attempt on the part of de Faria to recover the business he had lost to Bombay merchants. The plan to restore Peres da Silva's authority failed and brought about de Faria's bankruptcy in 1838.[92]

The diversion of larger quantities of Malwa opium to Bombay after 1831 did not immediately benefit the Company since private merchants, Indian and European, were able to retain a substantial share of the earnings from the trade. On the eve of the Opium War the Company's net profit on a chest of Bengal opium was on an average ten times (Rs.1250) the duty levied on each chest of Malwa opium.[93] The difference was large even when it is conceded that the cost price of Malwa opium was more than that of Bengal opium. Part of this share went to Indian merchants, but by the beginning of the 1840s growing problems of remittance from China coupled with the decline of indigenous shipping reduced the opportunities for capital accumulation available to the business class of Bombay.[94]

Nevertheless, opium opened up new possibilities for placing a hinterland at the disposal of Bombay. Various restrictions imposed on the export of Malwa opium from western India, beginning with the regulation of 1805, however inhibited the employment of the port's capital. Till almost 1831 the non-economic means employed to check Malwa opium trade only delayed Bombay's search for a hinterland by driving this lucrative enterprise away from the port and into independent, indigenously controlled avenues.

Right since the beginning of the nineteenth century Bombay merchants had large stakes in opium. Opium restrictions had forced them to break out of the confines of Bombay and participate in an active smuggling trade in partnership with Malwa, Gujarat and Rajasthan business groups. Bombay traders could not possibly afford to give up such an important field of investment. They therefore went in for opium smuggling in a big way. The Bombay authorities had often pointed out to the supreme government that the capital at hand in Bombay would not be easily inclined to withdraw 'from this profitable trade' though Bombay merchants 'would, of course, much prefer buying every chest of opium in a fair and open manner, to the course they were by our measures compelled'.[95]

It was private, particularly indigenous, enterprise that took the lead in making Bombay the centre of the economic activity of western India. For its own survival Bombay's merchant class had to make the opium (and cotton) supplying areas of western and central India into a hinterland for Bombay. Towards the end of the 1820s the Bombay government too, largely for reasons of revenue initially (though one should not ignore the traditionally strong links between the Bombay merchants and the Bombay government), was prepared to assist in this effort. Calcutta, to which the Bengal monopoly was of paramount concern, actually delayed the emergence of Bombay as the main centre for organizing the colonial plunder of western and central India.

It was almost inevitable that with the removal of restrictions on Malwa opium in 1831 and the concomitant expansion of trade in the commodity, spatially capital should have got concentrated at Bombay while western and central India fast became its hinterland. This spatial concentration was irresistible given that opium was primarily a commodity of external trade and Bombay with its institutional infrastructure was the most convenient location that could be available to indigenous enterprise for conducting the opium trade.

Opium provided to the Bombay bourgeoisie an important source of accumulation. This accumulation, together with the capital which had become available through a very strong indigenous presence in the commercial activity of western and central India, could then be channelized into industrial development at Bombay. This would take capitalist development in Bombay to a new level through making it a centre of industrial production.

Problems notwithstanding, the mood among Indian businessmen in Bombay was buoyant during the 1830s and early 1840s. The confidence that such a mood would have generated is reflected in the growth of business in Bombay. The ranks of the indigenous trading community in Bombay had swelled. The 1792 *Bombay Directory* lists names of a little less than fifty leading Indian businessmen from various communities – 'Gentoo Caste', 'Persic Caste', and 'Mussulman'.[96] The *Gazetteer of Bombay City and Island* gives a slightly lower figure for 1805, 40 leading non-European (Parsi, Hindu, Armenian and Bohra) firms at Bombay.[97] By 1846 there were at least 140 leading Indian merchants, sarrafs and bankers at Bombay.[98] Apart from the China trade, Bengal trade, shipping, coastal trade in western India, etc., Indians were engaged in a variety of trades in the city during the 1840s as auctioneers, bakers, confectioners, cabinet-makers, coach and palanquin builders, 'Europe' shopkeepers, gunsmiths, horse-dealers, printers and publishers, shipbuilders, watchmakers, wine-merchants, and tailors.[99] Some, though very few, were also to be found as directors of banks and insurance companies. In the early 1840s Jamsetjee Jejeebhoy was one of the six directors of the Bank of Bombay;[100] Juggonath Sunkersett was among the eight deputy chairmen of the Bank of Western India;[101] Framji Cowasji was one of the three trustees of the same bank;[102] Jamsetjee Jejeebhoy, Juggonath Sunkersett, Bomanji Hormasji and Framji Cowasji were on the committee of management of the Government Savings Bank at Bombay Castle;[103] and Manockji Nusserwanji was one of the directors of the Bombay Fire Assurance Company.[104]

During the latter half of the nineteenth century the major contradictions between indigenous enterprise and colonial interests at Bombay were played out in the arena of industry. The resistance of the early nineteenth century ensured continued participation of indigenous enterprise at Bombay, symbolized by Indian control over the city's cotton textile industry founded in the 1850s.

## Notes

[1] A typical example is Gillian Tindall's *City of Gold: The Biography of Bombay* (London, 1982).

[2] 'The British worked well with the Parsees of Bombay, ... who seemed to think more or less in the European manner, and were the first natives in India to play cricket ...'. James Morris, *Pax Britannica: The Climax of an Empire* (Harmondsworth, 1981), p.148. In his authoritative history of Indian cricket ('as distinct from cricket in India') Ramachandra Guha also notes that 'the first Indians to play cricket were the Parsis of Bombay', c. 1830s. However he brings out the contestations that were involved, revealing that 'the discriminatory tendencies of Empire had come to clash directly with the levelling tendencies of cricket'. Ramachandra Guha, *A Corner of a Foreign Field: The Indian History of a British Sport* (London, 2002), pp.11-12; 20-22.

[3] Om Prakash, 'European Commercial Enterprise in Pre-Colonial India', *The New Cambridge History of India*, Vol. II, 5 (Cambridge, 1998), p.201.

[4] Ibid., p.230.

[5] Ibid., p.282.

[6] Ibid., pp.282-283.

[7] Ibid., pp.327-328.

[8] Whereas it is difficult to estimate the earnings of Company officials from opium in the period immediately preceding the changes introduced by Hastings, the magnitude may be gauged from the £534,009 profit that the monopoly (then in its infancy) brought to the Company during Hastings's tenure. D.E. Owen, *British Opium Policy in China and India* (New Haven, 1934), p.37, n.42.

[9] J.B. Lyall, 'Note on the History of Opium in India and the Trade in it with China', *Royal Commission on Opium*, Vol VII (London, 1895), Appendix A, p.12; and R.M. Dane, ibid., Appendix B, p.37.

[10] Reporter general on external commerce, to J.A. Grant, secretary, Bombay Govt., 6 May 1803, NAI, SRBC, 3/30 June 1803.

[11] 'Minute' by Francis Warden, chief secretary, Bombay Govt., 30 April 1823, NAI, SRBC, 56/12 June 1823.

[12] Royal Commission on Opium, Vol. VI, p.27; also R. Fergusson, officiating advocate general, Fort William, to H. Mackenzie, secretary, Govt. of India, 30 July 1817, NAI, SRBC, 18/8 August 1817.

[13] Fort William to Bombay Govt., 30 June 1803, NAI, HD, Misc. Letters, 271.

[14] The western districts of present-day Madhya Pradesh, bound by Rajasthan and Gujarat in the west and the Narmada in the south. The main railway line running between Gwalior and Bhopal roughly marks the eastern extremity of Malwa.

[15] Cf. Habib, Atlas, p.38, and sheet 9 B indicating opium-growing areas of Malwa during the Mughal period.

[16] *The Book of Duarte Barbosa*, tr. M.L. Dames, Vol. II (London, 1921), p. 231. The opinion of Garcia da Orta, the great early sixteenth century Portuguese botanist who lived for several decades at Goa (and, incidentally had been granted large holdings in Bombay), that the opium exported from Cambay was chiefly obtained from Malwa is cited in George Watt, *A Dictionary of the Economic Products of India*, Vol. VI, 1, (London, 1972), p.34.

[17] Francis Warden dated the growth of trade in Malwa opium to the 1770s. Warden, 'Minute', NAI, SRBC, 30 April 1823, 56/12 June 1823.

[18] A.M. da Cunha (ed.), *Sir Roger de Faria: Notas Genealógicas e Biográficas* (Nova Goa, 1928), p.5.

[19] Ibid., p.3.

[20] GSAP, CM, 1296, fol. 213.

[21] GSAP, CM, 1295, fol. 152. This was to lead to a dispute later as to the status of de Faria at Macao.

[22] Celsa Pinto, *Trade and Finance in Portuguese India: A Study of the Portuguese Country Trade, 1770-1840* (New Delhi, 1994), pp.54-56, 78.

[23] XCHR, Mhamai Papers, file 1816-1828.

[24] J.F. Pereira to Warden, 15 July 1805, NAI, SRBC, 6/19 June 1806.

[25]  XCHR, Mhamai Papers, 'Borrador' (daybook), 1800-1801. The day book contains copies/drafts of several letters addressed to Jose Francisco Pereira at Bombay.

[26]  The Camotim firm also had links with Daya Ram Dulabha. Cf. letter to Doarama Durlobo, Damao, dated 21 May 1800, ibid.

[27]  *East India Register*, 1819, 1820, 1821.

[28]  C. Schuyler, envoy at Goa, to John Adam, 8 and 9 May 1815, NAI, SRBC, 24/26 July 1815; deposition of the Tendal of the pattamar Bhowany, 5 May 1815, enclosed in ibid; letter of Roger de Faria, 26 February 1817, XCHR, Mhamai Papers, file 1816-1828.

[29]  Pinto, *Trade and Finance*, p.74. On Miguel de Lima e Souza and his relationship with the East India Company see Nightingale, *Trade and Empire*, passim.

[30]  'Passaporte concedido pelo Governo do Estado em 20 de Agosto de 1810', GSAP, Monções do Reino, 205 B, fol. 704.

[31]  Letters of de Faria dated 21 May 1816 and 26 February 1817, XCHR, Mhamai Papers, file 1816-1828.

[32]  Enclosure 12 to letter dated 12 January 1829, GSAP, Monções do Reino, 205B.

[33]  Letter of de Faria dated 26 February 1817, XCHR, Mhamai Papers, file 1816-1828.

[34]  Letter dated 8 March 1817, XCHR, Mhamai Papers, file 1816-1828.

[35]  Da Cunha, *Roger de Faria*, p.5.

[36]  Ibid.

[37]  Pinto, *Trade and Finance*, pp.57-58.

[38]  Owen, *British Opium Policy*, p.85.

[39]  *Royal Commission on Opium*, Vol. VI, p.52.

[40]  For details see Amar Farooqui, *Smuggling as Subversion: Colonialism, Indian Merchants and the Politics of Opium* (Delhi, 1998), pp.18-19.

[41]  See ibid., pp.19 and 92ff.

[42]  Cf. D.F. Karaka's influential *History of the Parsis*, first published in 1884 (reprinted Delhi, 1986), Vol. II, chapter II and p.245.

[43]   Calculated from list in Farooqui, *Smuggling as Subversion*, Appendix A.i.b, pp.181-184.

[44]   Karaka, *History of the Parsis*, Vol. II, p.57; Dobbin, *Urban Leadership*, p.11; Amalendu Guha, 'More about Parsi Seths: Their Roots, Entrepreneurship and Comprador Role, 1650-1918', Centre for Studies in Social Sciences, Occasional Paper 50 (Calcutta, 1982), mimeo, p.24.

[45]   G.A. Natesan (compiled), *Famous Parsis* (Madras, 1930), pp.1-2; J.R.P. Mody, *Jamsetjee Jejeebhoy, the First Indian Knight and Baronet (1783-1859)* (Bombay, 1959), pp.10-11. I have relied on the dates given in Mody's book as these are based on more rigorous research than earlier biographical accounts.

[46]   Natesan, *Famous Parsis*, p.4.

[47]   *Bombay Courier*, 11 January 1800.

[48]   Ibid.

[49]   Mody, *Jamsetjee Jejeebhoy*, p.11.

[50]   Ibid.

[51]   In a letter written to the Chinese Hoqua Hong at Canton Jamsetjee Jejeebhoy states, 'you will be grieved to hear of our friend Merwanjee's death which took place some time in September last, his loss is I may say deeply and deservedly regretted by all who had the pleasure of appreciating his amiable disposition'. Letter dated 31 March 1831, NAI, Jamsetjee Jejeebhoy Letterbooks, microfilm, reel 1.

[52]   Natesan, *Famous Parsis*, p.4.

[53]   There is a graphic account of the entire episode in Karaka, *History of the Parsis*, Vol., II, pp.79-88.

[54]   Siddiqi, 'Business World', p.195.

[55]   Mody, *Jamsetjee Jejeebhoy*, p.15.

[56]   Cunha Rivara quoted in da Cunha, *Roger de Faria*, p.5.

[57]   Mody, *Jamsetjee Jejeebhoy*, p.32.

[58]   Ibid.

[59]   Consultation dated 14 August 1817, MSAM, Customs Revision Committee, Diary 187.

[60] Power of Attorney dated 7 November 1818, MSAM, Misc. Portuguese Records, 1819.

[61] Jamsetjee Jejeebhoy and 62 others to M. Elphinstone, governor, Bombay Presidency, 18 October 1820, MSAM, Customs Revision Committee, Diary 188. This is a copy of the petition forwarded to Henry Shank, president of the committee and does not contain the names of the other sixty-two signatories.

[62] Letter of James Matheson dated 3 June 1821, JMA, Out Correspondence, Misc. Early, C1/4 (James Matheson Letterbook, 1820-1821).

[63] Letter of Jamsetjee Jejeebhoy dated 24 April 1824, JMA, In Correspondence, Bombay, microfilm, reel 17, 63.

[64] The firm Charles Magniac existed from 1820-1825. Between 1825 and 1832 it operated under the name Magniac and Co. William Jardine and James Matheson joined Magniac and Co. as partners in 1825 and 1827, respectively. Magniac and Co. became Jardine, Matheson in 1832. The prior contacts between Jardine and Jamsetjee must have played a role in cementing the bonds between Magniac and Co. and Jamsetjee after Jardine became a partner in the firm in 1825. The most exhaustive account of the early history of Jardine Matheson is to be found in W.E. Cheong, *Mandarins and Merchants: Jardine Matheson & Co., a China Agency of the Early Nineteenth Century* (London, 1979).

[65] Letter of Matheson dated 10 March 1821, JMA, Out Correspondence, C1/4.

[66] Letter from Roger de Faria and Co. dated 1 January 1825, JMA, In Correspondence, Bombay, microfilm reel 17, 144.

[67] Letter of Matheson dated 19 April 1821, JMA, Out Correspondence, C1/4.

[68] Natesan, *Famous Parsis*, pp.7-8.

[69] Letter from M. de Vitre dated 7 May 1832, JMA, In Correspondence, Bombay, reel 25, 2551.

[70] Ibid.

[71] Board of Customs, Salt and Opium to governor general, 3 June 1826, NAI, SRBC, 18/22 June 1826.

[72] The following discussion on smuggling of Malwa opium is based mainly on Farooqui, *Smuggling as Subversion*, chapter V.

73   J. Ago. da Silva to Motichund Amichund, 14 April 1825, JMA, In Correspondence, Bombay, reel 17, 184.

74   Ibid., 185.

75   Letter of Jamsetjee dated 7 May 1825, ibid.

76   Letter of William Jardine dated 2 June 1825, ibid.

77   Ibid.

78   Ibid.

79   Siddiqi, 'Business World', p.209

80   Letter of J.H. Crawford dated 26 March 1824, JMA, In Correspondence, Bombay, reel 17, 23.

81   See Guha, 'Parsi Seths as Entrepreneurs', p. 109.

82   Guha, 'More about Parsi Seths', p.17.

83   The Wadias are a classic case of the failure of Indian shipowners to develop a modern shipbuilding industry at Bombay due to colonial constraints despite the availability of capital and requisite skills. Guha points out 'that even for the master ship-builders, the scope of growing into full-fledged industrial entrepreneurs in their own line was more limited than what is generally believed'. Guha, 'More about Parsi Seths', p.15.

84   Govt. of India resolution, 19 June 1829, NAI, Foreign Department (Political), 70/19 June 1829.

85   John Malcolm, governor, Bombay presidency, 'Minute', 6 May 1830, NAI, SRBC, 23/7 September 1830.

86   Ibid.

87   Abstract dated 22 August 1844, MSAM, Revenue Deptt., Vol. 95/1652 (1844).

88   Owen, *British Opium Policy*, p.101, n.61.

89   Claude Markovits, *The Global World of Indian Merchants, 1750-1947: Traders of Sind from Bukhara to Panama* (Cambridge, 2000), p.41 and n.23. For an evaluation of the evidence see J.Y. Wong, 'British Annexation of Sind in 1843: An Economic Perspective', *MAS*, Vol. XXXI, 2 (1997), pp.226; 234-237.

90   Farooqui, *Smuggling as Subversion*, p.157.

[91] A.F. Moniz, *Notícias e Documentos Para a História de Damão, Antiga Provincia do Norte*, Vol. III (Bastora, 1910), pp.54 ff; 187, 231; 241.

[92] For details see Teotonio R. de Souza, 'Rogério de Faria: An Indo-Portuguese Trader with China Links', Artur Teodorio de Matos and Luís Filipe F.R. Thomaz (ed.), *As Relações entre a Índia Portuguesa, a Ásia do Sudleste, e o Extremo Oriente* (Macao/Lisbon, 1993), pp.309-319.

[93] Govt. of India to Bombay Govt., 27 September 1837, NAI, SRBC, 6/27 September 1837.

[94] Cf. Siddiqi, 'Business World', pp.202-208; 211-217; Guha, 'More about Parsi Seths', p.17.

[95] Malcolm, 'Minute', 6 May 1830, NAI, SRBC, 23/7 September 1830; also Bombay Govt. to Supreme Govt., 5 December 1829, NAI, SRBC, 14/12 January 1830.

[96] *Bombay Directory, 1792*, reproduced in James Douglas, *Bombay and Western India*, Vol. I (Bombay, 1893), chapter XII.

[97] *Gazetteer of Bombay City and Island*, Vol. I, p.414.

[98] *BCGD*, 1846, pp.167-169.

[99] *BCA*, 1842, iii, pp.8-10; *BCA*, 1843, iii, pp.8-10; *BCA*, 1844, ii, pp.66-68; and *BCGD*, 1846, p.170.

[100] *BCA*, 1843, p.29.

[101] Ibid., p.31; *BCA*, 1844, ii, p.89.

[102] *BCA*, 1843, p.31

[103] *BCA*, 1843, p.32; *BCA*, 1844, ii, p.90.

[104] *BCA*, 1843, p.25. The Parsis had taken the lead in the development of joint-stock banks in Bombay during the 1840s. See Guha, 'More about Parsi Seths', pp.25-26.

# URBAN DEVELOPMENT IN
# EARLY VICTORIAN BOMBAY

The distinctiveness of the western Indian colonial situation had its impact on the urban development of Bombay as a capitalist port city. From an urban sociological perspective early Victorian Bombay was representative not so much of a colonial city with its colonial/indigenous spatial dualism, but was an easily recognizable capitalist city with class differentiation determining its spatial pattern.

In the early nineteenth century Bombay was fast acquiring an easily recognizable capitalist face. The city was well maintained in parts, it was squalid and congested in others. Population was expanding; there was growing functional specialization and division of labour; relations of the market were penetrating day to day life; and class differentiation was cruelly apparent. Urban development in nineteenth century Bombay has to be placed within the wider framework of the development of capitalism and the intervention of colonialism. It goes without saying that colonial rulers brought to urban development in India certain features which were inherited from the historical evolution of cities in the metropolis.[1] At the same time it has to be borne in mind that such features were inescapable in so far as colonial rule drew various urban centres in India into a network of capitalist relations. Indian cities on which the British left their imprint became less or more capitalist cities depending upon the extent to which capitalism was able to develop/not develop in them or in the region/s in which they were located.

In Bombay, just as in Calcutta, Madras, Simla, Ootacamund or Pondicherry a pre-colonial city did not confine the colonial city. The organization of space in colonial Bombay was therefore unencumbered by historical usage. In Delhi, Lucknow, Ahmad-abad, Pune and other cities with a pre-colonial past the pattern of colonial urban development had to take into account space which had already been historically appropriated.[2] It was often difficult to internally modify the usage of this space to suit colonial requirements: the colonial city had to be located externally. The example of Delhi is instructive. Here colonial rulers created two 'external' cities, at different points of time. One was in the middle of the nineteenth century, especially after 1857-58, when the area outside Kashmiri Gate was developed as an exclusively British 'civil lines'. Beyond the 'civil lines', troops were quartered near the Ridge. This was the time when a belligerent Delhi was being subdued after the 1857 Revolt. Before 1857 the British had shown a preference for the area lying north of Lal Qila. The residency, St. James' Church, Ludlow Castle and Metcalfe House were all located in this direction, close to the centre of the old city. As in the case of Hyderabad the location of the residency was intended to facilitate a live intercourse with the indigenous elite.[3] There was a radical departure after 1857-58. Under the influence of military planners such as Robert Napier, who had 'cleaned up' Lucknow, the colonial civil and military establishment was now completely detached from the walled city. During the latter half of the nineteenth century 'urban Delhi conformed to the classical model of "native city", cantonment and "civil station"',[4] so characteristic of the colonial urban tradition in towns with a pre-colonial history. Then, after the decision to transfer the capital of British India from Calcutta to Delhi in 1911, a new external city was built, this time on a grand scale, on the southern outskirts of the old city. Raisina village was to house symbols of occidental despotism and ample space intervened between the new city and the old. The one did not easily impinge upon the other and the ivory tower feeling of the viceregal residence was complete.

In those cities which evolved largely as a result of British initiative, colonial urban development did not merely have to be the other of indigenous settlement. As there had been no initial appropriation of space in these cities, it was possible for the colonial rulers to take up the most favourable locations which then became the nucleus and raison d'etre of the city as a whole. Here too it would be inaccurate to talk of a uniform pattern. In the major colonial port cities— Calcutta, Madras and Bombay— where defence against external enemies had initially been an important consideration,[5] a fortified European settlement became the starting point of development. The earliest model was provided by Portuguese factories with their defensive walls and looking out towards the sea. In these cities, however, a live economic and administrative contact with various indigenous groups was vital for the East India Company. Hence it was not feasible that the non-indigenous part of the city be isolated, permitting no interaction. Indigenous groups had to be allowed some access to a few prime locations either within or in the vicinity of the fortified settlement. In hill-stations where the British did not look forward to any intercourse with the 'natives', and which had been built at a time when British rule was relatively secure, far greater freedom in creating a non-indigenous environment was possible.[6]

There is, therefore, no such thing as colonial urban development in the abstract. Various urban centres were products of specific historical conjunctures. The sanitaria apart, for strictly speaking their historical role was very limited, urban centres of colonial India reflected variations in the level of capitalist development in different parts of the country. Spatial organization therein was indicative of the relative strength or weakness of indigenous groups and their capacity to intervene in the control of urban space. The urban development of Bombay has to be seen in this context.

Here one might draw attention to the distorted nature of urban development which colonial rule set in motion. Urban centres developed or patronized by the metropolis in colonies often failed to generate economic activity concomitant with their expansion, since much of this expansion was often not the result of an organic growth but was related to specific colonial economic, military, administrative, strategic, and/or political considerations. The hegemony of the colonial power placed it in a position to intervene arbitrarily in according primacy to a particular urban centre in a given region so that frequently artificial, imposed and unintegrated urban development took place.

The nucleus of early British Bombay was the Fort area, situated along the south-eastern tip of the original island of Bombay and facing the harbour. The Fort had developed around Bombay Castle that dated back to the Portuguese days. The Castle had been used as a residence-cum-godown by the Company and was gradually fortified. The settlement which grew up around it was later protected by a wall built in several phases during the mid-eighteenth century. The area enclosed by this wall came to be known as the Fort.[7]

The security which the Fort provided, coupled with its location near the harbour and docks, made it not only a commercial and administrative centre but a residential area as well. Eventually the Fort became hopelessly overcrowded and as we shall see it required a major fire in 1803 for some planning to be contemplated. The physical geography of the part of Bombay in which the Fort was located permitted expansion only in one direction, that is, towards the north. South of the Fort, the narrow strip of Colaba and Old Woman's Island had very limited space. To the west of the Fort there was some open space, the esplanade.

The esplanade was usually left unbuilt in colonial cities as a matter of convention, mainly for military reasons. It was of the nature of a clearing outside the Fort 'intended to prevent any person approaching the town without being seen from the citadel'.[8] The grand public buildings on the eastern edge of Bombay's esplanade were not constructed before the latter half of the nineteenth century.

With growing congestion in the Fort area, the appropriation of land within it primarily for commercial use, and with relatively greater security, Malabar Hill (with its extension, Cumballa Hill) at the south-western tip of the island became the fashionable residential area for the colonial elite. This was the more so after the governor shifted his residence from Parel to a most enviable site on the edge of Malabar Hill, overlooking the sea. This area was not too far from, yet not too near, the hub of activity in the city.

North of the Fort and separated from it by the esplanade was the main indigenous habitation zone. This zone was, until its subsequent further expansion to the north, almost within walking distance from the Fort and the docks where many of the Indians found employment. As business grew and got attracted to the Fort area, it made sense to live in this zone and thereby cut down on commuting time, a crucial consideration in an age when mass rapid public transport was non-existent. As it is, Bombay being an island, expansion in all directions was out of the question. Moreover, during the eighteenth century the salt flats in the centre of Bombay island were still in the process of being reclaimed, delaying the dispersal of population over this area. When in the latter half of the nineteenth century Parel and the area beyond it towards the north and upto the waterfront in the east developed as an industrial centre, population got concentrated along a diagonal running roughly from Dongri to Worli. This diagonal was more or less equidistant from the factories lying to the north and north-east of it and the commercial centres lying south and south-east of it. All this was of course before Salsette was seriously developed into a suburb of Bombay.

Some figures pertaining to the population of Bombay during the early nineteenth century are available which, though they may not be entirely accurate, do give us a broad idea of the demographic situation in this period. It was estimated in 1814 that the permanent population of the island 'may now be taken at 1,80,000 souls'.[9] The floating population was an additional 60,000. Thus the total was about 240,000 persons.[10] This was an appreciable increase over the figure for the last quarter of eighteenth century. In 1780 the population of Bombay was estimated to have been 47,170.[11]

Already by the turn of the century there was a marked increase in the population of the city or, at least, that was the general impression of contemporary observers. Maria Graham noted in 1809, shortly after the influx caused by a famine in the

Konkan and Deccan, 'I was informed that Bombay contains upwards of two hundred thousand inhabitants'.[12]

The influx seems to have been temporary. It did not by itself make Bombay a major centre of either production or consumption. When in 1805 Fort William was considering a plea made by the Bombay government for abolishing town duties, reference was made 'to the limited consumption of the Town', owing to which 'the amount realized from the Town duties at that Presidency' were 'too inconsiderable'.[13] There was consequently no reason why the request should not have been acceded to. The supreme government thus recommended that the duties be abolished.[14]

What the movement of population towards the city does confirm however is that Bombay's coastal links were stronger than its (overland) links with its interior. This enabled it to avoid serious food shortages. Foodgrains could be imported via the sea. Bengal was a major supplier during the Konkan famine of 1803 (see Appendix B). Naturally a number of people afflicted by the famine sought succour in privileged Bombay.

There is a likelihood that early population figures were inflated. This is made apparent by a census of Bombay taken in 1826 which put the total population at only 162,570, i.e. lower than the estimates for 1814.[15] By 1833 the population had risen to 234,032,[16] a crude rate of growth of 5.34% per annum. Another census, taken in 1849, recorded 566,119 inhabitants.[17] By 1864, 816,542 persons resided in the city.[18] In other words the rate of growth of population between 1849 and 1864 had declined to 2.47% per annum. Although as D.R. Gadgil had pointed out in the context of population statistics for Bombay that earlier counts appear to be over-estimates,[19] the general impression one gathers is that the 1830s and 1840s were a period of very rapid increase as compared to the 1850s and 1860s. The overall rate of growth between 1826 and 1849 was 5.57% per annum. This rate of growth was higher than that which occurred from 1849-1864 (2.47% per annum), as well as for the overall period from 1826 to 1864, 4.34% per annum.

By the end of the first quarter of the nineteenth century the bulk of Bombay's population was to be found in Dongri, Byculla, Mahim, Girgaum and of course the Fort. Dongri and Byculla with 47,359 and 31,083 inhabitants respectively accounted for as much as 48.25% of Bombay's total population in 1826.[20] However, the Fort area was still the most densely populated part of Bombay. It contained 13,611 persons in 1826[21] (as against 10,801 in 1813),[22] who resided in 1219 houses, that is, about 11.2 persons to each house (Table 4).

### Table 4
### Persons per house in Bombay, 1826

| Area | Persons per house |
|------|-------------------|
| Fort | 11.2 |
| Dongri | 8.7 |
| Byculla | 7.2 |
| Malabar Hill etc. | 6.9 |
| Girgaum | 5.8 |
| Mazagaon | 5.25 |
| Colaba | 4.95 |
| Mahim, including Worli etc. | 3.6 |

Source: *Calculated from 'Census of Bombay, 1826'.*

These figures do not include the military and floating population of Bombay, which was put at 10,000 and 20,000 respectively.[23] It is unlikely that the floating population of Bombay would have easily found accommodation in the Fort, Colaba or Malabar Hill. This group would have mainly been dispersed over the indigenous zone thereby pushing up the density of those areas.

W.H. Sykes observed with reference to the 1849 census of Bombay that the 'native town east of Bhendy Bazar contains more than two-fifths of the entire population of the Island'.[24] Sykes further drew attention to the immense excess of males over females in Bombay, there being 354,090 males to 212,029 females in 1849.[25] One of the reasons for this was that 'Bombay comprises a large number of seamen, workmen in dockyards, factories etc. who come without their wives'.[26]

Bombay was eventually placed in an arbitrarily privileged position due to colonial intervention. Hence it was able to attract a large population which could not always be efficiently utilized given Bombay's lack of a hinterland and its weak links with the interior. Consequently there was bound to be a section of the population which could not be provided steady employment. At peak times, particularly during the sailing season, some of the casual labour was able to find work in dockyards, cotton screws etc. but this labour would have been redundant for the remaining part of the year when they would be forced to leave the island or possibly look around for means of self-employment. Warden's impression was that one-fourth of the population of the island was 'floating' in 1814. This floating population comprised 'Camatees, Ghatees, Carwas, Maharattas, Arabs, Persians and Goa Portuguese, a great part the sea faring men, with many Parsees'.[27] These temporary, many of them from the west coast especially the Konkan area, residents remained in Bombay a few years, hoarded their earnings, and 'having saved from two to three hundred rupees, return to their native country, where they obtain as much land as they require'.[28] Much of this casual labour therefore retained a strong connection with land, something which would have inhibited the process of creating a large wage-earning class. Till such time as colonialism tightened its grip on the western Indian countryside, the possibility of falling back on land would have definitely prevented complete degradation of this floating population of Bombay. This is in sharp contrast to, say, the casual labour of London, which had really no land to return to, and was, therefore, forced to submit to the most inhuman living conditions.[29] In England, of course, the appropriation of the countryside was extremely drastic and has never exactly been duplicated elsewhere.[30] In western India too the rural option was closed for urban dwellers once colonial exploitation led to a deteriorating agrarian situation. In Bombay city itself the strength of indigenous enterprise, the transfer of the opium trade to the city, the vitality of commercial activity and industrial development did help in partially overcoming the problem. In 1826 the floating population of Bombay was, as we have noted, placed at 20,000, a sudden drop as compared to the estimates of 60,000 for 1814. Too much should not be read into the decline of this component of the population within the space of just twelve years. Firstly, total population placed at 240,000 in 1814 was 162,570 according to the count of 1826, which in turn may be explained to some extent by an overestimation of the earlier figure. Secondly, we are completely in the dark about the precise definition of the category 'floating population' for both years. In the absence of information about what criteria were adopted for classifying someone as belonging to this category, a proper comparison between these two figures cannot be made. Suffice it to say that there was a sufficiently large floating population in the city during the first quarter of the nineteenth century, and the non-permanent component may have been showing a downward trend during the late 1820s as a result of new avenues that became available with increased economic activity in this period.[31]

With the the rapid growth of the city it was necessary to ensure that those who flocked to the city did some work, even if it was something most dismal requiring much labour and yielding but a pittance. To be absolutely idle and unemployed could mean taking to vagabondage and even a life of petty-thievery. In a city where traditional ties did not exist, particularly as Bombay had no pre-colonial past—the lack of such ties being underscored by the penetration of market relations—little support from the community was forthcoming for anyone who had the misfortune of being totally without means of livelihood. Such a person might constitute a threat to property: s/he might rob, steal, burgle. It is not surprising therefore that there were stringent provisions in Bombay 'for sending aliens off the island', particularly those who 'live idle without work'.[32] Such persons could 'be committed to jail, be flogged, and, upon a second conviction, upon production of the former record, they may be sent off the island'.[33]

The division of labour and production for exchange which capitalism presupposes and the encapsulation of this division of labour within urban space leads to a major contradiction: while urban space must be appropriated for functions related to the accumulation of capital, this accumulation of capital is a negation of self-sufficiency and requires the apportioning of space for classes which live only by their labour. The contradiction becomes sharper as economic activity gets concentrated in urban areas due to the convenience of finding there the necessary labour as well as the infrastructure— finance, banks, credit facilities, transport, technical expertise — needed for the accumulation of capital (which in turn reinforces this concentration). There is a tendency to apportion as little space as possible to the poor. This is not merely a matter of land value, which is bound to go up with such concentration and which as adding to the cost of production is somewhat offset by the abundance of labour within the urban area, but is also a matter of not providing adequate amenities for the poor. It is, however, desirable to have a growing population of wage-earners who are willing to sell their labour power since this allows a large residual section which can be both casually engaged and recruited if there is any attempt on the part of any group of workers/wage-earners to exert pressure for improving their living conditions.[34]

It should not surprise us that initially in view of Bombay's marginality during the seventeenth century and most of the eighteenth the shortage of urban land did not become a major problem till the early nineteenth century, except in the case of the Fort area. As we have noted, the Fort provided security; it was the main administrative and commercial centre; it was located adjacent to the harbour; and the seven islands of which Bombay was formed were still in the process of being integrated so that it was not feasible for urban settlement to be widely dispersed further north and west.

The year following the transfer of Bombay from the Crown to the East India Company, an official proclamation (which remained inoperative) stated that all acquisition of land by individuals prior to 1661 had proceeded from imperfect right.[35] A few year later, in 1674, an important step was taken in the direction of the development of land as private property. Recognition was given to possession of all the land then occupied by individuals, subject however to the condition that occupants were liable for military service. The tenure was regarded as feudal.[36] What is significant is the added provision that occupants could not be deprived of their holding without compensation.[37]

These arrangements were apparently applicable essentially to the Fort area, for in some of the other parts of Bombay (Girgaum, Chowpatty, Walkeshwar, Cumballa Hill and Mahim) a tax called 'pension' was levied.[38] This was of the nature of an agricultural tax on garden or rice land computed 'at so much per wheel for irrigation'.[39] Although, according to Warden, it would appear 'that a very small part of the Island was in a state of cultivation' at this date, in effect these areas were not adequately urbanized.[40]

In 1718 the pre-capitalist form (military service) which rent had taken in the Fort area was converted to a tax expressed in money, referred to as quit-rent.[41] This was really a tax for a service rendered by the state, rather than a rent on land. No argument in terms of a superior right to land was however put forth. Quit-rent was legally only a reimbursement for expenses incurred for erecting fortifications.[42] To put it differently, it was a tax for providing security. Since it was the Fort and the surrounding area which benefited from these fortifications, the tax applied to land in the Fort, Colaba, the 'Black' Town and the New Town. The 'Black' Town and the New Town were the indigenous zones lying respectively north and north-west of the Fort.[43]

By the 1730s colonial elites began asserting superior rights to land. This was obviously the easiest way to exclude, or at least limit indigenous access to land. Indians were preempted by a discriminatory taxation policy. A resolution of 1731 made a distinction 'between the English and black [!] inhabitants'.[44] This policy did not deter Indians from acquiring landed property on an extensive scale in Bombay, a situation to which the strength of indigenous enterprise contributed in no small measure. In 1803, as we shall see, another attempt was made to undermine indigenous control over land in the Fort. The attempt proved futile. By the second decade of the nineteenth century there seems to have been an all round strengthening of property rights along capitalist lines with reduced colonial arbitrariness. Such colonial arbitrariness acts as a serious limitation to the proper exercise of bourgeois right by discriminating essentially along racial rather than class lines. In 1814 Warden advocated the further strengthening of private property.[45] In 1814 itself the right of tenants to inherit and alienate land was also accepted.[46]

The Fort area being the focus of the economic world of the city, the actual outcome of the conflict between colonial rule and indigenous capitalism in Bombay was mirrored in that small strip of land. Just as the British were unable to completely overcome opium smugglers so too they could not prevent Indian merchants from gaining a foothold in the Fort area. Moreover, if the nascent indigenous bourgeoisie was an important participant in the commercial life of the city its desire to be in close proximity to that infrastructure which colonial interests had spatially concentrated in the Fort was but natural. It would not be out of place to state here 'that in 1707-8 the greater part of the ...Fort was private property; ...[ and ] that, for the purchases made from 1707-8 to 1758-9, it became the Company's and was subsequently *transferred to individuals*' (emphasis added).[47] What this implies is that since we find Indians as substantial owners of property in the Fort by the beginning of the nineteenth century, they must also have been involved in these large-scale purchases made during the latter half of the eighteenth country. Investment in real estate increased in this period: 'the greatest portion of the property will be found to have been created since the year 1758'.[48]

In 1803 a major fire broke out in the Fort.[49] D.E. Wacha recalled in his reminiscences that he had heard from his grandmother 'in the Fifties what a terrible catastrophe it was. At the time the news of fire, large or small, was one to fill the citizens with extreme consternation, for it meant, in nine cases out of ten, total destruction of life and property'.[50] The fire wiped out more than four hundred buildings, occupying an area of nearly 30,000 sq yards.[51]

The fire became an occasion for trying to oust Indians from the Fort. This is understandable when we consider that land values in the Fort escalated rapidly after the fire. Just before 1803 the price of land had been on an average from eight to twelve rupees per square yard. After 1803 it ranged between Rs.16 and Rs.30 per square yard.[52]

Following the fire a Town Committee was appointed ostensibly 'to investigate the nature of tenures' in tracts laid waste by the calamity.[53] Under the garb of examining the nature of tenures in the Fort, the Committee sought to obstruct reconstruction of indigenously owned buildings.[54] This was met with stiff resistance by Indians. They were not prepared to accept this threat to their right to reside and own property in the Fort. Though the Town Committee attempted 'to carry their plans into effect, as well by threats as by persuasion [sic]', the 'natives ultimately succeeded in their opposition, and in the object of rebuilding on their old foundations'.[55] Significantly, and perhaps keeping the larger picture in view, even the Court of Directors concurred in 'permitting a native town within the Fort'.[56]

We find Hormasji Bomanji constructing his family residence in the Fort during the first decade of nineteenth century at an estimated expense of one and a half lakhs of rupees.[57] Ardaseer Dady owned four building in the area.[58] Motichund Amichund had his premises in Bazargate Street.[59] Besides, Cursetji Manockji, Kesowdass Ransordass, Moosa Mapla and Pestonji Bomanji also owned land in the Fort during the first quarter of the nineteenth century.[60] Of the eight largest landowners in the Fort, six were

Indians. The biggest property owners were Pestonji Bomanji (15,598 sq yards) and Hormasji Bomanji (12,146 sq yards).[61] Coercion having been unsuccessful, Indians were induced in this period to exchange land held in the Fort for large tracts of ground in Salsette, which was still in an undeveloped state.

Within the Fort itself there was some segregation. Indians clustered around the northern part of it whereas 'in the southern part ... congregated the official European population'.[62] After 1772 there was a definite bar on Indian's settling in the southern section of the Fort.[63] In the north, Indians tended to live in small localities constituted along caste or occupational lines.[64] Hardly any planning had gone into the development of the Fort.[65] In the late 1820s it conveyed the impression 'of a large irregular village than of a town'.[66] Writing in 1809, Maria Graham had observed that the Fort was 'Dirty, hot, and disagreeable, particularly the quarter near the bazar-gate, owing to the ruins of houses which were burnt down some time ago, and have never been removed; but new buildings are in many places rising on the broken fragments of the old, so that the streets are become so uneven as to render it disagreeable if not dangerous, for carriages to pass through them'.[67]

The Bazar Gate was located at the northern end of the Fort, in the area where the indigenous inhabitants resided. The houses of Indians within the walls were 'closely crowded together, very high, and most built of wood'.[68] The fact that they were made of wood must have added to the risk of fire. If even after the fire of 1803 wood continued to be used so extensively as building material, bricks and stone must have been expensive and difficult to procure. As it is the expenses of building were great, owing partly to the high cost of labour, and accounted 'for the apparently moderate profit enjoyed by the builder'.[69] The wooden houses in the fort 'with their wooden verandahs, venetian blinds, and heavy sloping roofs, covered with tiles' had a 'Swiss rather than Oriental appearance' for a casual observer.[70] The absence of chimneys in these houses caused 'them to look as if they were so many warehouses'.[71]

There were certain physical limits beyond which it was not possible to go on adding buildings within the Fort area. By the end of 1820s 'substantial buildings [extended] to very nearly three miles from the Fort'.[72] Some efforts were made to relieve the congestion in the Fort area, though not always with much success. In the period after the fire, Indians had been asked 'to limit their houses in respect to height and taking off from each front a portion of ground for widening the streets'.[73] Then in 1839, legislation pertaining to building construction in Bombay, Act No.XXVIII, laid down that no building with a height extending beyond 50 feet could be erected within the walls of the Fort.[74] Yet as late as the 1860s, the authorities noted that, 'The Fort has hitherto been strictly limited by its ramparts..., but while its lateral extension has been prevented, there has been no restriction as to the number of stories that might be added to houses'.[75]

South, north and west of the Fort there was some open space. This could not be used for expansion partly for physical and partly for strategic reasons. Colaba and Old Woman's Island were not fully integrated with Bombay till quite late.[76] Colaba was initially a cantonment area, although towards the beginning of the nineteenth century it was opened up for civilians.[77] The proximity of Colaba to the Fort, its spaciousness and fine view soon made it prime land. In 1805 the East India Company paid Rs.60,000 for purchasing eight houses in Colaba.[78]

The large expanse of the esplanade merging with the sea on one side and with the indigenous zone on the other provided, apart from its strategic importance which has already been alluded to, much needed escape from the claustrophobia of the Fort. It was a place where one could go for a breath of fresh air, for some recreation and exchange of gossip. This is where Parsi boys began playing cricket. Even in the third quarter of the nineteenth century the esplanade retained its calm. Despite the railway, textile mills, the cotton boom and rise in population the pace of life was still unhurried along the esplanade. Wacha gives a most vivid description of pleasant evenings spent here during the 1850s:

> ... squatting groups would be seen merrily playing games of cards .... Refreshments were also vended. The only refreshment was the sugarcane, stripped of its bark and cut into small cylindrical pieces which again would be subdivided into four. A large number of vendors, also Parsis, selling this fruit... moved from group to group....[79]

Further,

> the grounds on which now stand the Post Office... and the High Court were also utilized for recreation purposes, but evidently it was dedicated to the *shettia loque* or the wealthier of the Parsi community. Members of this class, too, frequented the maidan and had their little groups – only these were a little more exclusive....[80]

It is pertinent that the esplanade was not appropriated exclusively for the use of the colonial elite.

Malabar Hill comes closest to King's concept of 'colonial settlement' in colonial urban centres as an area where the European civilian population resided and from which indigenes were almost entirely excluded.[81] Indians, however, owned a lot of land in this area as well. Framji Cowasji 'owned a few bungalows there'[82] as did Hormusji Cursetji, son of Cursetji Manockji, one of the prominent owners of land in Bombay whose property in the Fort has already been referred to above.[83] Kemp and Co. had their medical dispensary in Malabar Hill in premises rented from Hormusji Cursetji's widow, Meheribai.[84]

Owning property in Malabar Hill was one thing but residing there was another. In the 1840s 'the healthy eminence of Malabar Hill was quite untenanted by any Parsees' or, for that matter, by other Indians.[85] Houses owned by Parsis 'were without exception occupied by Europeans'.[86] When in 1848 Meheribai decided to shift to Walkeshwar in this part of Bombay, the step caused an outcry which obviously had sexist overtones as well: 'The Parsee Punchayet the body conducting the social governance of the Parsee community, gave it out as their grave opinion, that it was anomalous for a Parsee lady to live in such an out-of-the-way locality'.[87] This exclusive quarter extended almost upto Breach Candy at the northern extremity of Cumballa Hill. Breach Candy soon became 'the general rendevouz of the English community, where they met to settle the politics of the island, and to discuss the affairs of the day...'.[88]

Class differentiation and social segregation in Bombay was most sharply delineated in moving from the rarefied atmosphere of Malabar Hill, Walkeshwar, Cumballa Hill and Breach Candy to the Native Town north of the Fort. Here too as the demand for housing increased with the rise in population during the early nineteenth century, the value of land went up. Those who owned land took 'all possible advantage of the area in their possession by building to its full depth' and 'raised floor upon floor'.[89] Moreover, 'some owners of plots of ground which have a frontage such only as may have been sufficient for a huckster's stall before the street attained to its present importance, have built with this small frontage, but with a greatly disproportioned depth, houses of many floors'.[90] Consequently the overcrowding was oppressive. Dwellings were at times constructed by filling a wooden framework with brick and mortar or rubble masonry. In the poorer streets the walls were made entirely of wood. This rendered the structures insecure as was 'shown in the many accidents that have resulted from falling houses in the ten years ending with 1862. Besides many being maimed, there were 69 killed in that time'.[91]

Congestion in the indigenous zone was in direct proportion to the concentration of economic activity in the Fort. In the absence of an even spacing of economic activity, those who had only their labour power to sell could not be widely dispersed but had to be as close as possible to the area which could provide them work. As Indian enterprise too tended to get concentrated in the Fort, reinforcing the economic significance of the area, the spatial disorientation of Bombay was ensured. We have also noted that Bombay during the first quarter of the nineteenth century could not utilize its large population efficiently. The fact that the Fort area was not really a producing zone, rendered Bombay's labour even more underemployed. This meant that many were forced to be self-employed as petty-shopkeepers, hawkers and vendors. It was possible to sustain oneself to a limited extent on this kind of activity since Bombay's wage-earners had to buy the necessities of daily life. Maria Graham recording her impressions of a visit to a Bombay bazar wrote:

> Here you see grain of every description heaped in earthen jars; there, sweetmeats of all sorts and shapes, .... Further on, fruits and vegetables are laid out to the best advantage; then you come to the paung, or betel leaf, nut and chunam, ready for chewing, or the separate materials; beyond are shops for perfumes, linens, oils, toys, brass and earthenware....[92]

This variety of economic activity related to vending articles of daily necessity became so much that the Bombay authorities imposed a tax on shops and stalls. Act XI of 1845 provided 'that it shall be lawful for the collection of Land Revenue of Bombay to make a Quarterly Assessment on each and every shop and stall within the Island of Bombay and Colaba'.[93] The types of shops and stalls listed convey some idea about the nature of business in articles of daily necessity: Apothecary (Country); Bakers; Bread Sellers; Betelnut Sellers; Curds and Cream Sellers; Darners; Dinner Leaves Sellers; Onion, Garlic, Ginger, Potatoes and Yam Sellers; Pickle Sellers; Rice Sellers; and Tea and Sugar Sellers.[94]

The Native Town had some autonomous economic activity, but this being on too small a scale and at a very low level, ultimately dependence on the Fort was crucial. This desperate dependence on the Fort would have been another factor responsible for the disproportionately large concentration in that area.

Such a situation in the main indigenous zone and the Fort obviously led to unhygienic conditions. A.H. Leith, as deputy inspector-general of hospitals in Bombay, in a report of 1864 on the sanitary conditions in the city, reported that in a particular street 'the houses on each side were of two or three floors, and the various rooms were densely peopled, and the floors of the verandahs were fully occupied, while to eke out the accommodation in some of the verandahs there were *charpaees* or cots slung up and screened with old matting to form a second tier of sleeping places for labourers that were employed in the day'.[95]

In one of the *chals* (Bombay's typical multi-storeyed working/lower class residential compounds with shared facilities) that Leith visited, he found

> ...in a narrow unpaved court, which was wet with the waste water of a well round which the people were bathing, there was a cesspit full of filth: in the same enclosures there was a row of necessaries behind which there was an unbuilt trench full of fluid excreta and foul water, the over-flowings of which passed along the base of the wall surrounding the mouth of a well that was but four feet

from the privy. This well supplied its owner's household with drinking water. In this Chal there were ten cholera deaths'.[96]

Elsewhere he was led to latrines where

'baskets which cannot retain liquid are used under the privy-seats, and those privies have a flat floor, and... as is often the case, not even a basket is used, and a sweeper never visits the place, but the accumulated soil is left to flow out on the pavement of the gullee...'.[97]

Under the circumstances, frequent outbreaks of epidemics particularly of cholera were only to be expected. In the early nineteenth century three major outbreaks of cholera occurred: in 1831-32, in 1848-49 and in 1853-54. In 1849 cholera deaths amounted to 18,036 while in 1854 approximately 20,000 people were estimated to have died of the disease.[98]

The abysmal sanitary conditions prevailing in the Fort, and to an even greater extent in the Native Town, were bound to result in the contamination of drinking water thus leading to cholera and other contagious and water-borne diseases. The shortage of water supply compounded the problem. Even British inhabitants had at times to procure water from distant sources. An entry of 1825 in Lady West's journal states, 'we had sixty-three bottles filled yesterday at the Caves of Elephanta for drinking'.[99] Repeated monsoon failures between 1824 and 1850 led to the drying up of the 136 public wells and tanks on which the inhabitants were completely dependent for their supply of water. By 1854 only eight of these wells and tanks contained good, potable water.[100]

In the 1850s a major project for the supply of water was under consideration in Bombay. The project was to be financed largely through an increased house tax.[101] Mariam Dossal's detailed study of this project has shed light on an important facet of this issue. The wealthier Indians led by Jamsetjee Jejeebhoy, were not favourably inclined towards the project as they would have had to 'submit to a heavy tax for such works'.[102]

The matter was one of class interests. Privileged indigenous groups, with their own private wells, were not keen to provide amenities to the deprived sections if there was to be increased taxation. It might seem a contradiction that whereas the affluent Indians tried to stall the move, it is the colonial state which was in this case taking the initiative in improving civic amenities. Enzo Mingione in his work on capitalist urban problems has pointed out that, 'As the taxation system is based on residents,... any change discourages capital accumulation because it becomes – one way or another – a direct taxation of economic activities'.[103] From the point of view of the capitalist class of Bombay the question was whether it would be prepared to bear the high costs of providing amenities for the poor. In an overall situation of colonial constraints to accept this responsibility would have further reduced their scope for capital accumulation. One must recall here that indigenous investment in Bombay's housing and real-estate was extensive.

Needless to say, for the bulk of the Indian inhabitants of the city, life in the Native Town and Fort during the early nineteenth century must have been a miserable one. This was all the more so as with the growing stability of British rule the European inhabitants of Bombay moved to the more fashionable areas of Colaba and Malabar Hill, abandoning the Fort to commerce, and middle and upper class Indians. Of course there were still European residents in the southern part of the Fort, but what one is referring to is the general trend.[104]

North and central Bombay did not come into their own until the industrial era. Just north of Dongri, along the sea, was Mazagaon. In 1826 it had a population of 4696.[105] Maria Graham referred to it at the beginning of the century as 'a dirty Portuguese village'.[106] Till very recently there was 'a very Portuguese air to Mathapakardy, the small settlement that nestles quietly in the heart of busy Mazagaon'.[107] Not being very far from the Native Town or even the Fort, and due to its importance as a ship-building centre, Mazagaon was a settlement of some importance in the early nineteenth century.

Several portions of north and central Bombay had been reclaimed only during the early eighteenth century.[108] Having been reclaimed largely at government expense, the land had been let out to individuals, mainly Indians, for improvement. Most of this land consisted of salt marshes, and was designated *foras*.[109] *Foras* (lit. 'out of doors') denoted rent 'paid by a cultivator or person permitted to occupy ground for the purpose of improving it'.[110] Large tracts of Byculla, Parel, Worli, Mahim, Dadar and Matunga were *foras* lands.[111] With the rising value of land in Bombay, the government tried to undermine the rights of holders of *foras* at the beginning of the nineteenth century.[112] At the same time the Company contemplated an increase in rent, 'but the holders of these grounds strongly resisted'.[113] Eventually "the measure of increasing the rents was suspended, and the matter referred to the Hon'ble Court of Directors in 1815".[114] The matter was settled for the time being with titles of those 'persons who were in possession in the year 1744' being recognized in perpetuity.[115]

The question of rights was reopened in the 1830s. In 1836 the construction of a major thoroughfare in central Bombay, passing through *foras* lands, was projected.[116] This thoroughfare, Grant Road, now Maulana Shaukat Ali Road, forming a junction with Girgaum Road was to have an east-west alignment. In 1838, work on the road commenced and the *foras* lands through which it passed were acquired without any compensation being paid.[117]

Rapid expansion of the city and the construction of Grant Road further increased the value of land in central Bombay. In the 1840s we find leading merchants like Juggonath Sunkersett and Bomanji Homasji investing in land in the Tardeo and Grant Road area.[118]

Parel, where also several *foras* holdings were located, had been a favoured resort in the eighteenth century. The governor had his residence here which, with preference being increasingly shown for Malabar Hill, was abandoned during the course of the nineteenth century. The threatened northward expansion of the indigenous zone and the overall southward shift of the European residential zone (Colaba and Malabar Hill) completed the eclipse of Parel. Some upper class Indians did continue to have their country residences in Parel during the nineteenth century, the most well-known being Pestonji's 'Lal Baug'. The famous Lowji Wadia family, it may be mentioned in passing, had been given *inam* or cess-free grants in Parel and adjoining Naigaum in 1783.[119] In the latter half of the nineteenth century this area became mainly an industrial zone.

Mahim had been an important settlement since the Portuguese days and was the most thickly populated area in north Bombay at the beginning of the nineteenth century. Mahim was estimated to have 13,726 inhabitants in 1760.[120] In 1826 the population of Mahim (including Worli) was 17,713.[121]

During our period Salsette, the large northern neighbour of Bombay, was still a backwater. It is only towards the end of the nineteenth century, particularly with the improvement of communications, that Bombay began to spill over into Salsette. Salsette was to become an 'umland': the 'umland' of a city being that portion of the surrounding country which is linked with the city as a centre.[122] As Bombay's physical geography permitted only northward expansion, the merger of Salsette with Bombay was inevitable.

Salsette had been one of the earliest additions to the Bombay presidency. It was 'at the time of its acquisition much depopulated and scantily cultivated'.[123] With the growth in demand for food in Bombay, Salsette was sought to be better cultivated. Leases were granted on favourable terms to attract settlers.[124] Bishop Heber refers to vegetables grown on Salsette being brought to the Bombay market c. 1820s.[125] At the same time Heber noted that the island was 'strangely unimproved having no towns except Tannah and Gorabunder (the first of which is indeed a neat and flourishing place, the other not so much better than a poor village)'.[126] He went on to say: 'This neglected and uncivilized state of Salsette is all the more remarkable, ... because the neighbourhood of Bombay, and the excessive price of provisions there, would seem to lead to the cultivation of every inch of ground'.[127] Finally, Heber remarked that, 'The population, however, poor as it is, and chiefly occupied in fishing, amounts to 50,000, a number which might be trebled if cultivation were extended at anything like the rate which it has been done in Bengal'.[128]

The main reason why the capacity of Salsette remained underutilized was that cultivation called for a large investment. According to a report of 1836 one of the major obstacles in the development of Salsette was 'the nature of the soil itself, which is not capable of being made productive without the constant and unceasing aid of expensive appliances'.[129]

There is one other sense in which Salsette was tied to the economy of Bombay in the early nineteenth century. It provided a field for investment in land. Several prominent merchants of Bombay had been granted holdings in Salsette in this period, some of which had been given in exchange for land in the Fort.[130]

Ardaseer Dady had been granted the villages of Malhar, Dysar, Magatney, Tulsi, Areyn, Eksar, Kanari and part of Pahadi in lieu of land in the Fort. Hormasji Bomanji had similarly been given the villages of Kurlen, Maroli, Asalpay, Kolikalian, Mohili, Parajpor and Shahar (collectively referred to as the Kurla estate).[131] Some of the other prominent landowners in Salsette were: Cursetji Manockji (Anik); Dhakji Dadaji (Varsavay); Framji Cowasji (Poway estate), Jamsetji Bomanji (Vila Parla, Jhu); Cursetji Cowasji (Goregaum); Ratanji Edulji (Gatkopar)); Krushnarao Raghunath (Borvday); and Luxmon Hurrichanderji (Chincholi).[132]

It would seem that much of the indigenous investment in Salsette was of a speculative nature. It was rare for Bombay merchants to go in for investment in agriculture.[133] One of those occasional instances is that of Framji Cowasji who tried to introduce scientific agriculture on his Poway estate. The relatively greater stability of indigenous enterprise in Bombay did not incline Indian merchants towards large investments in agriculture. Urban real-estate, over which they already had significant control (Pestonji Bomanji boasted to Maria Graham 'that he received not less than £15,000 a year in rents and his brother received nearly as much'), held greater attraction for them.[134]

The development of capitalism in Bombay was not only expressed in the specific spatial pattern of the city but also in the availability of certain facilities and services so characteristic of a capitalist city, especially a major administrative and commercial centre. To some extent such facilities were the outcome of Bombay's privileged position within the colonial scheme of things: systematic appropriation requires an infrastructure.

In the context of early nineteenth century colonial Bombay the growth of specialization could at times be deceptive, especially at the lower level. The non-manufacturing nature of Bombay's economy in this phase must have, as we have already noted, led to a number of people becoming hawkers, vendors, small-shopkeepers, carriage drivers, palanquin-bearers, and construction workers. Unfortunately our information is limited to those services and facilities which were usually availed of by the Europeans or upper class Indian inhabitants of Bombay.

There were, by the late 1830s and early 1840s several hotels, coffee-shops, eating houses and confectioneries in the city. In contrast to the situation at the beginning of the century when Maria Graham lamented that 'there is but one tavern in Bombay and... that is by no means fit for the reception of ladies',[135] and a similar statement by Mrs. Elwood in the late 1820s that '... it is most singular that there are no hotels to which a lady could with propriety go',[136] several hotels came up between the late 1830s and early 1850s: Victoria Hotel, Hope Hall, British Hotel, Madam Costa, Royal Family and Benson Hotel.[137] The hotels proclaimed their respectability by announcing the availability of accommodation for 'Families and Gentlemen'.[138] These hotels were not exclusively European-owned but had indigenous involvement as well. Victoria Hotel in Apollo Street had, for instance, Nasserwanji Cooverji as one of its owners.[139]

The Shop and Stall Tax of 1845 differentiated between two kinds of eating houses. Eating houses for Europeans on which the quarterly assessment was Rs.4/-, and ordinary eating houses (apparently for non-Europeans) on which the tax was one rupee.[140] The implied segregation is significant. A similar type of establishment referred to in the list pertaining to the Shop and Stall Tax is the coffee shop.[141]

The taste for European confectionery was not limited to British residents alone, but had percolated down to some indigenous sections as well. Indians were also engaged in vending this kind of confectionery. Dhunjeebhoy Framjee's bakery was one of the well-known establishments in the early forties.[142] In the forties itself Rustomji Framji was one of the two 'ice-confectioners' in Bombay, the other being a European.[143] Wacha tells us of 'a Parsi who had a bakery in Barrack Lane' in the 1850s. A shop, familiarly known as Bahadurji's Bakery, 'had the custom of the rich and middle class Parsis', while another 'humbler confectioner of the Military Store Lane supplied the needs of the lower classes'.[144]

At a more everyday level, we have seen that the supply of foodgrains to Bombay had been taken care of largely through sea-borne trade. For highly perishable commodities like vegetables and fruits, however, local production was necessary. Among the vegetables grown in Bombay were brinjals, *bhindi*, various types of gourds, and sweet potatoes.[145] Peas and beans were also grown but were of 'indifferent quality'. Not much success had attended planting of cabbage, carrots and turnips. There was some specialized horticulture also.[146] Bombay was famed for its onions;[147] Mazagaon for its mango.[148] Finally, some rice was still cultivated on the island in the early nineteenth century.[149]

As settlements got dispersed over the island, the demand for transport also increased. Buggies, carriages, carts and palanquins were available for hire.[150] The rise in their number necessitated legislation to regulate such transport. Act No.IV of 1841 allotted specified parking places (stands) for public vehicles and palanquins.[151] The phenomenal rise in utilization of road space can be gauged from the following statement pertaining to the 1860s:[152]

> As many as 598 carriages in addition to bullock carts were counted passing along the Bhendy Bazar in one hour, and as there

were 4,500 foot passengers for whom there are no footpaths, the
danger to life is very great and many accidents occur.

Finally, there was the seamier side of Bombay. Petty crime in the
city was the obverse of a flourising commerce in opium and other
commodities. J.P. Grant, judge of the King's Court in Bombay,
delivering an address in 1828 stated that, 'Daring robberies are
perpetrated within the walls of a fortified town by gangs—goods
are conveyed to the ramparts and lowered down by ropes attached
to the guns of the fort'.[153] Crime had brought with it a police force.
Following a regulation of 1812 the police establishment consisted
of a senior magistrate, a junior magistrate, and a superintendent
of police. There were three police divisions—Fort, Byculla and
Mahim—each with a head constable.[154]

This police force, along with the judiciary, became the
instrument for safeguarding bourgeois property against pilferage
and theft. Punishment was harsh: confinement, banishment,
torture. In the Petty Sessions 'the infliction of punishment by
rattan' was 'a very common sentence' during the 1820s.[155] Lashing
was 'attended with extraordinary severity, drawing blood at every
stripe, and sometimes taking off with it small pieces of flesh'.[156]
While upper class Indians served on juries or were appointed
justices of the peace, the poorer sections were the victims of such
savage methods of punishment. The scars caused by lashing which
were 'never obliterated but by death' could be observed 'on many
a native as he toils along the streets of the town under the burden
of a palanquin'.[157] The pillory was very much in use in Bombay
at the turn of the century and this brutal form of punishment
remained an option till at least 1834.[158]

Magistrates exercised their authority in a most arbitrary
manner, carrying terror 'into the poorest hovel by his peons
dispersed over the island'.[159] Appeal against such arbitrariness

was not easy. In a Kafkaesque episode, 'on the 6th of October 1817, a man ... was sentenced to hard labour till he should find securities. Under this sentence he remained in jail till July 1823, a period of six years, when he died in jail'.[160]

Michel Foucault speaks of the 'severe repression of illegality', out of all proportion to the offence, in bourgeois society: 'The development of ports, the appearance of great warehouses in which merchandise was stored, the organization of huge workshops... also necessitated a severe repression of illegality. The way in which wealth tended to be invested, on a much larger scale than before, in commodities and machines presupposed a systematic, armed intolerance of illegality'.[161]

The development of capitalism in Bombay was thus equipped to protect bourgeois property against petty-crime while, in a world of topsy-turvy morality, colonial and indigenous enterprise operating from the city merrily peddled opium to the Chinese.

## Notes

[1]  Cf. A.D. King, *Colonial Urban Development* (London, 1976), pp. 36ff.

[2]  On Delhi see ibid. and Narayani Gupta, *Delhi Between Two Empires, 1803-1931* (Delhi, 1981). Some other specific case studies on the subject are K.L. Gillion, *Ahmadabad, A Study in Indian Urban History* (Berkeley, 1978); Veena T. Oldenburg, *The Making of Colonial Lucknow, 1856-1877* (Princeton, 1984); Meera Kosambi, *Bombay and Poona: A Socio-Ecological Study of Two Indian Cities, 1650-1900* (Stockholm, 1980); Pamela Kanwar, *Imperial Simla: The Political Culture of the Raj* (Delhi, 1990); and Mariam Dossal, *Imperial Designs and Indian Realities: The Planning of Bombay City, 1845-1875* (Bombay, 1991).

[3]  Cf. William Dalrymple, *White Mughals: Love and Betrayal in Eighteenth Century India* (New Delhi, 2002) for the social and cultural implications that the location of the residency had in Hyderabad.

[4]  King, *Colonial Urban Development*, p.228.

[5]　See, Partha Mitter, 'Architectural Planning and other Building Activities of the British in Madras, Bombay and Calcutta c.1630-c.1757' Dilip Basu (ed.), *The Rise and Growth of the Colonial Port Cities in Asia* (Berkeley, 1985), p.192.

[6]　See Amar Farooqui, 'Colonial Get-Away', Review of Pamela Kanwar, Imperial Simla, *EPW,* Vol. XXVI, 50 (1991), pp.2874-5.

[7]　Dulcinea Correa Rodrigues, *Bombay Fort in the Eighteenth Century* (Bombay, 1994), p. 82.

[8]　King, *Colonial Urban Development*, p.88

[9]　Warden, *Landed Tenures*, p.73. In Warden's view the population of Bombay in the first quarter of the eighteenth century 'did not exceed ten thousand souls'. Ibid., p.24.

[10]　Ibid.

[11]　James Campbell, *Materials Towards a Statistical Account of the Town and Island of Bombay*, Vol.III (Bombay, 1894), p.525.

[12]　Maria Graham, *Journal of a Residence in India* (Edinburgh, 1813), p.4.

[13]　Fort William to Bombay Govt., 29 December 1805, NAI, HD, Misc. Letters.

[14]　Ibid.

[15]　'Census of Population of Islands of Bombay and Colabah taken in... 1826', *Transactions of the Bombay Geographical Society*, III (Bombay, 1840), p.72.

[16]　*BCA*, 1838, p.121.

[17]　W.H. Sykes, *On the Census of the Islands of Bombay and Colabah* (Bombay, 1852), p.1.

[18]　A.H. Leith, Report on the Sanitary State of the Island of Bombay, *BGS*, new series, 80 (Bombay, 1864), p.46.

[19]　D.R. Gadgil, 'Origins of the Modern Indian Business Class: An Interim Report', New York, 1959, reprinted in S. Brahme (ed.), *Writings and Speeches of Prof. D.R. Gadgil on Economic Problems* (Pune, 1981), p.325, n.7. On the shortcomings of early census figures for Bombay see also Dossal, *Imperial Designs*, pp.24-5.

[20]　'Census of Bombay, 1826', Table 1.

[21]　Ibid.

[22] Campbell, *Materials*, Vol.III, p.526.

[23] 'Census of Bombay, 1826', Table 1.

[24] Sykes, *Census*, p.1.

[25] Ibid.

[26] Ibid., p.2.

[27] Warden, *Landed Tenures*, p.101.

[28] Ibid.

[29] See Gareth Stedman Jones, *Outcast London* (Harmondsworth, 1976), especially, chapter III.

[30] Cf. Enzo Mingione, *Social Conflict and the City* (Oxford, 1981), p.91.

[31] However in the 1860s the population of Bombay was 'supposed to be formed in great part of immigrants as nearly one-half of the casualties reported in the Mortuary Returns were of persons whose birthplace was elsewhere'. Leith, *Sanitary State*, p.24. A great influx of labourers took place between 1860 and 1890 and in the 1880s only 23% of the total population claimed the island as their birthplace, *Imperial Gazetteer of India*, Vol.VIII (Oxford, 1907), pp.411-12. There was considerable fluctuation in this period. The cotton boom of the early 1860s caused a growth in population, followed by a decline which was reflected in the census of 1872. Dossal, *Imperial Designs*, pp.210-1.

[32] Sir E. West, Chief Justice, King's Court, Bombay, 'Charge to the Grand Jury', 1825, in F.D. Drewitt, *Bombay in the Days of George IV: Memoirs of Sir Edward West*, second revised edition (London, 1935), pp.188-9.

[33] Ibid.

[34] Cf. Manuel Castells, *The Urban Question* (London, 1977), and D. Harvey, *The Urbanization of Capital: Studies in the History and Theory of Capitalist Urbanization* (Oxford, 1985).

[35] Character of Land Tenures and System of Survey and Settlement in the Bombay Presidency, *BGS*, new series, No.278 (Bombay, 1908), p.15.

[36] Ibid.

[37] Ibid.

[38] Ibid., p.16.

[39]  Ibid.

[40]  Warden, *Landed Tenures*, p.24.

[41]  *Character of Land Tenures*, p.15.

[42]  Ibid.

[43]  Cf. Ibid., p.16.

[44]  Resolution of November 1731, quoted in Warden, *Landed Tenures*, p.80.

[45]  Ibid., p.86.

[46]  *Character of Land Tenures*, p.15.

[47]  Warden, *Landed Tenures*, p.107. Rodrigues observes that at the beginning of the eighteenth century most of the land within the Fort was private property since settlers had been encouraged 'to occupy whatever land they pleased'. However in the second quarter of the century land was being forcibly taken over by the Company and the indigenous settlers were pressurized into moving out of the area, 'so that much of the private land given away to the early settlers was re-possessed'. Rodrigues, *Bombay Fort*, pp. 84-85.

[48]  Ibid., p.78.

[49]  Cf. Ibid., p.36.

[50]  D.E. Wacha, *Shells from the Sands of Bombay* (Bombay, 1920), p.67.

[51]  Warden, *Landed Tenures*, p. 36; Rodrigues, *Bombay Fort*, p. 96.

[52]  Warden, *Landed Tenures*, pp.92-3.

[53]  Ibid., p.36.

[54]  Ibid., p.43.

[55]  Ibid.

[56]  Ibid.

[57]  Ibid., p.46.

[58]  Ibid., p.98.

[59]  Wacha, *Shells from the Sands*, p.102.

[60]  Warden, *Landed Tenures*, pp.96-9.

[61]  Ibid., pp. 96-97.

[62]  W. Hamilton, *East India Gazetteer*, Vol. I (London, 1828), Vol. I, p.258; Wacha, *Shells from the Sands*, p.104.

[63]  Rodrigues, *Bombay Fort*, p. 95.

[64]  Cf. Mariam Dossal, 'Signatures in Space: Land Use in Colonial Bombay', Sujata Patel and Alice Thorner, (eds.), *Bombay: Metaphor for Modern India* (Bombay, 1995), p. 94.

[65]  Cf. Leith, *Sanitary State*, p.9; also, Mitter, 'Architectural Planning', p.191.

[66]  Mrs. Elwood, *Narrative of a Journey Overland From England... to India ... in the years 1825, 26,27,28 etc.*, Vol.II (London, 1830), p.89.

[67]  Graham, *Journal*, p.12.

[68]  Ibid., pp.11-12.

[69]  Warden, *Landed Tenures*, p.100.

[70]  Elwood, *Narrative*, Vol.II, pp.89-90.

[71]  Ibid., p.90.

[72]  Hamilton, *East India Gazetteer*, Vol.I, p.258.

[73]  Warden, *Landed Tenures*, p.43.

[74]  *BCGD*, 1849, p.265.

[75]  Leith, *Sanitary State*, p.9.

[76]  Cf. Kosambi, *Bombay and Poona*, pp.91-2.

[77]  Ibid.

[78]  Hamilton, *East India Gazetteer*, Vol.I, p.434.

[79]  Wacha, *Shells from the Sands*, pp.85-7.

[80]  Ibid., pp.89-90.

[81]  Cf. King, *Colonial Urban Development*, p.33.

[82]  Dosebai Cowasjee Jessawalla, *The Story of My Life* (Bombay, 1911), p.49.

[83]  Ibid.

[84]  Ibid.

[85] Ibid.

[86] Ibid.

[87] Ibid.

[88] Elwood, *Narrative*, Vol.I, pp.378-9.

[89] Leith, *Sanitary State*, p.9.

[90] Ibid.

[91] Ibid., p.10.

[92] Graham, *Journal*, pp.33-4. Tobacco and arrack were also important articles of consumption among the poorer sections of the population. See Warden, *Landed Tenures*, p.102.

[93] *BCGD*, 1849, p.252. 'Since 1827 the shop and stall tax had formed the backbone of Bombay's municipal finances. It was expected to pay for the costs of the municipal establishment, keep roads and tanks in repair and, since 1851, maintain a police force'. Dossal, *Imperial Designs*, p.66.

[94] 'Selected types of establishments liable for Shop and Stall Tax under Act XI of 1845', *BCGD*, 1849, p.252.

[95] Leith, *Sanitary State*, p.25. For a comprehensive discussion on Leith's report see Dossal, *Imperial Designs*, chapter 5.

[96] Ibid., pp.14-15.

[97] Ibid., p.13.

[98] Russel Aitken, *Report on the Main Drainage of Bombay*, 21 December 1866 (Bombay, 1866), p.29.

[99] Drewitt, *Bombay in the Days of George IV*, p.168.

[100] Mariam Dossal, 'Henry Conybeare and the politics of centralized water supply in mid-nineteenth century Bombay', *IESHR*, Vol. XXV, 1 (1988), p.86.

[101] Ibid., p.85.

[102] Ibid., p.87.

[103] Mingione, *Social Conflict*, p.52.

[104] Cf. Kosambi, *Bombay and Poona*, p.114.

[105] 'Census of Bombay, 1826'.

[106] Graham, *Journal*, p.6.

[107] *Bombay* (fortnightly), Vol. IX, 12 (1988).

[108] A.S. LeMessurier, 'Report on Foras Lands', 23 December 1843, Papers Connected with the Settlement etc. of the Foras Lands in Bombay, *BGS*, new series, No.3 (Bombay, 1854), p.2.

[109] Ibid., pp.2-3.

[110] Ibid., pp.6-7.

[111] *Character of Land Tenures*, p.16.

[112] LeMessurier, 'Report', pp.6-9.

[113] Ibid., p.9.

[114] Ibid.

[115] Ibid., p.11.

[116] Ibid., p.12.

[117] Ibid., p.13.

[118] 'Final Report of Foras Commissioners', Foras Papers, p.40.

[119] *Character of Land Tenures*, p.16.

[120] Campbell, *Materials*, Vol.III, p.525.

[121] 'Census of Bombay, 1826'.

[122] C. Rajagopalan, *The Greater Bombay: A Study in Suburban Ecology* (Bombay, 1962), p.19, n.2.

[123] Pestanji Jehangir, *Report on the Leasehold and Certain Other Villages in the Salsette Taluka of the Thanna Collectorate, 17 July 1872* (Bombay, 1875), p.1.

[124] Ibid.

[125] Bishop Reginald Heber, *Narrative of a Journey Through The Upper Provinces of India From Calcutta to Bombay*, Vol. II (London, 1828), p.185.

[126] Ibid., p.186.

[127] Ibid.

[128] Ibid, p.187. In 1827 the total population of Salsette island was estimated to be 53,255. *Transactions of the Bombay Geographical Society*, III, p.73.

[129] 'Report of Mr. Davies', March 1836, quoted in Correspondence Relating to the Conditions on which Certain Estates are held in the Salsette Taluka etc., *BGS*, new series, 180 (Bombay, 1886), p.15.

[130] Correspondence Relating to etc. Salsette, pp.11-13 and 125.

[131] Ibid., p.125.

[132] Ibid, pp.12-20, 76, 119-20, 125-6 and 141.

[133] Cf. Dobbin, *Urban Leadership*, pp.12-13.

[134] Graham, *Journal*, p.45. In the second decade of the nineteenth century Pestonji Bomanji's landed property was valued at Rs.424,500; that of Hormasji Bomanji at Rs.312,300; of Ardaseer Dady at Rs.385,431; of Cursetji Manockji at Rs.94,300; of Moosa Mapla at Rs.169,200; and of Kesowdass Ransordass at Rs.114,500. Warden, *Landed Tenures*, pp. 96-9.

[135] Graham, *Journal*, p.6.

[136] Elwood, *Narrative*, Vol.I, p.365.

[137] *BCA*, 1838, p.121; *BCGD*, 1842, Part III, pp.8-10; 1843, Part III, pp. 8-10; 1844, Part II, pp.66-8; and 1851, pp. 889-90.

[138] *BCA*, 1844, Part II, p.68.

[139] *BCA*, 1838, p.121.

[140] *BCGD*, 1849, p.252.

[141] Ibid.

[142] *BCA*, 1842, Part III, p.67.

[143] *BCGD*, 1849, p.948.

[144] Wacha, *Shells from the Sands*, p.90.

[145] Graham, *Journal*, p.24.

[146] Ibid.

[147] Elwood, *Narrative*, Vol.I, p.393.

[148] Ibid, p.388.

[149] Ibid, p.395; Graham, *Journal*, p.5.

[150] *BCGD*, 1849, p.254.

[151] Ibid., pp.254-5.

[152] Aitken, *Report on Main Drainage*, p.21.

[153] Drewitt, *Bombay in the Days of George IV*, p.275.

[154] S.M. Edwardes, *The Bombay City Police: A Historical Sketch, 1672-1916* (London, 1923), p. 23.

[155] West's 'Charge to the Grand Jury', Drewitt, *Bombay in the Days of George IV*, pp.191-3.

[156] Ibid., p.191.

[157] Ibid., p.194.

[158] Edwardes, *Bombay City Police*, p. 30.

[159] Ibid., p.202.

[160] Ibid., p.195.

[161] Michel Foucault, *Discipline and Punish: The Birth of the Prison* (Harmondsworth, 1985), p.85.

# BIBLIOGRAPHY

## Archival Sources

1. National Archives of India

Home Department, Miscellaneous Letters.

Foreign Department (Political) Consultations.

Jamsetjee Jejeebhoy Letter Books (microfilm).

Separate Revenue Branch Consultations (Opium).

2. Maharashtra State Archives, Mumbai

Customs Revision Committee Records.

Grain Scarcity Records.

Miscellaneous Portuguese Records.

Poona Residency, Inward Letter Books.

Revenue Department.

3. Goa State Archives, Panaji

Correspondência de Macau.

Monções do Reino.

4. Xavier Centre of Historical Research, Porvorim, Goa

Mhamai Papers.

5. Jardine Matheson Archives, University Library, Cambridge

In Correspondence, Unbound Letters, Bombay.

Out Correspondence, Private Letter Books.

## Other Sources

Russel Aitken, *Report on the Main Drainage of Bombay,* 21 December 1866 (Bombay, 1866).

Amiya K. Bagchi, 'Transition to British Indian Systems of Money and Banking, 1800-1850', *MAS,* Vol. XIX, no. 3 (1985).

Duarte Barbosa, *The Book of Duarte Barbosa,* tr. M.L. Dames, Vol. I (London, 1918); Vol. II (London, 1921).

*Bombay Calendar and Almanac / Bombay Calendar and General Directory.*

*Bombay Courier,* 1800.

*Bombay Times,* 1838.

Asa Briggs, *Victorian Cities* (Harmondsworth, 1977).

Anne Bulley, *The Bombay Country Ships, 1790-1833* (Richmond, 2000).

John Burnell, *Bombay in the Days of Queen Anne,* intro. and notes by S.T. Sheppard (London, 1933).

James Campbell, *Materials Towards a Statistical Accout of the Town and Island of Bombay,* Vol. III (Bombay, 1894).

'Census of Population of Islands of Bombay and Colabah taken in … 1826', *Transactions of the Bombay Geographical Society,* III (Bombay, 1840).

*Character of Land Tenures and System of Survey and Settlement in the Bombay Presidency, BGS*, new series, No. 278 (Bombay, 1908).

K.N. Chaudhuri, *The Trading World of Asia and the English East India Company, 1660-1760* (Cambridge, 1978).

W.E. Cheong, *Mandarins and Merchants: Jardine Matheson and Co., a China Agency of the Early Nineteenth Century* (London, 1979).

M.S. Commissariat, *A History of Gujarat*, Vol. II (Bombay, 1957).

*Correspondence Relating to the Conditions on which Certain Estates are held in the Salsette Taluka etc., BGS*, new series, No. 180 (Bombay, 1886).

A.M. da Cunha, ed., *Sir Roger de Faria: Notas Genealógicas e Biográficas* (Nova Goa, 1928).

J. G. da Cunha, *The Origin of Bombay* (Bombay, 1900).

Ashin Das Gupta, *Indian Merchants and the Decline of Surat, c. 1700-1750* (Wiesbaden, 1979).

—, 'Indian Merchants in the Age of Partnership, 1500-1800', Dwijendra Tripathi, ed., *Business Communities of India: A Historical Perspective* (New Delhi, 1984).

—, 'India and the Indian Ocean in the Eighteenth Century', Ashin Das Gupta and M.N. Pearson, eds., *India and the Indian Ocean: 1500-1800* (Calcutta, 1987).

Christine Dobbin, *Urban Leadership in Western India: Politics and Communities in Bombay City, 1840-1885* (London, 1972).

Mariam Dossal, 'Henry Conybeare and the Politics of Centralized Water Supply in Mid-Nineteenth Century Bombay', *IESHR*, Vol. XXV, no. 1 (1988).

—, *Imperial Designs and Indian Realities: The Planning of Bombay City, 1845-1875* (Bombay, 1991).

—, 'Signatures in Space: Land Use in Colonial Bombay', Sujata Patel and Alice Thorner, eds., *Bombay: Metaphor for Modern India* (Bombay, 1995).

James Douglas, *Bombay and Western India*, Vol. I (Bombay, 1893).

F.D. Drewitt, *Bombay in the Days of George IV: Memoirs of Sir Edward West*, second revised edition (London, 1935).

*East India Register.*

S.M. Edwardes, *The Bombay City Police: A Historical Sketch, 1672-1916* (London, 1923).

Mrs. Elwood, *Narrative of a Journey Overland from England ... to India ... in the Years 1825, 26, 27, 28, etc.* (London, 1830).

Amar Farooqui, *Smuggling as Subversion: Colonialism, Indian Merchants and the Politics of Opium* (Delhi, 1998).

Holden Furber, *John Company at Work* (Harvard, 1951).

—, *Bombay Presidency in the Mid-Eighteenth Century* (Bombay, 1965).

—, *Rival Empires of Trade in the Orient, 1600-1800* (Minneapolis, 1976).

*Gazetteer of Bombay City and Island*, 3 Vols. (Bombay, 1909).

B.G. Gokhale, *Surat in the Seventeenth Century: A Study in Urban History of Pre-Modern India* (Bombay, 1979).

Maria Graham, *Journal of a Residence in India* (Edinburgh, 1813).

Amalendu Guha, 'Comprador Role of Parsi Seths: 1750-1850', *EPW*, Vol. V, no. 48 (1970).

—, 'Parsi Seths as Entrepreneurs: 1750-1850', *EPW*, Vol. V, no. 35 (1970).

—, 'More About Parsi Seths: Their Roots, Entrepreneurship and Comprador Role. 1650-1918', Centre for Studies in Social Sciences, Occasional Paper No. 50 (Calcutta, 1982), mimeo.

Ramachandra Guha, *A Corner of a Foreign Field: The Indian History of a British Sport* (London, 2002).

*Gujarat State Gazetters, Surat District*, revised edition (Ahmedabad, 1962).

Irfan Habib, *An Atlas of the Mughal Empire* (Delhi, 1982).

W. Hamilton, *East India Gazetteer* (London, 1828).

David Hardiman, 'Elite Conflicts in a Trading Empire', *EPW*, Vol. XVI, no. 50 (1981).

Bishop Reginald Heber, *Narrative of a Journey Through the Upper Provinces of India from Calcutta to Bombay* (London, 1828).

*Imperial Gazetteer of India* (Oxford, 1907).

• Pestanji Jehangir, *Report on the Leasehold and Certain other Villages in the Salsette Taluka of the Thanna Collectorate* (Bombay, 1875).

Dosebai Cowasjee Jessawalla, *The Story of My Life* (Bombay, 1911).

D.F. Karaka, *History of the Parsis*, reprint (Delhi, 1986).

Anthony King, *Colonial Urban Development* (London, 1976).

J.J.C. Kol, *A General, Statistical and Historical Report on Portuguese India, Extracted in 1850 from Official Documents*, *BGS*, new series, No. 10 (Bombay, 1855).

Meera Kosambi, *Bombay and Poona: A Socio-Ecological Study of Two Indian Cities, 1650-1900* (Stockholm, 1980).

A.H. Leith, *Report on the Sanitary State of the Island of Bombay*, *BGS*, new series, No. 80 (Bombay, 1864).

*Maharashtra State Gazetteer, Greater Bombay District*, Vol. I (Bombay, 1986).

Claude Markovits, *The Global World of Indian Merchants, 1750-1947: Traders of Sind from Bukhara to Panama* (Cambridge, 2000).

P.J. Marshall, *East Indian Fortunes: The British in Bengal in the Eighteenth Century* (Oxford, 1976).

Enzo Mingione, *Social Conflict and the City* (Oxford, 1981).

Partha Mitter, 'Architectural Planning and other Building Activities of the British in Madras, Bombay and Calcutta c. 1630-1757', Dilip Basu ed., *The Rise and Growth of Colonial Port Cities in Asia* (Berkeley, 1985).

J.R.P. Mody, *Jamsetjee Jejeebhoy, the First Indian Knight and Baronet (1783-1859)* (Bombay, 1959).

A.F. Moniz, *Notícias e Documentos Para a História de Damão, Antiga Provincia do Norte*, Vol. III (Bastora, 1910).

James Morris, *Pax Britannica: The Climax of Empire* (Harmondsworth, 1981).

G.A. Natesan (compiled), *Famous Parsis* (Madras, 1930).

Pamela Nightingale, *Trade and Empire in Western India, 1784-1806* (Cambridge, 1970).

Om Prakash, *European Commercial Enterprise in Pre-Colonial India, The Cambridge History of India*, Vol. II, 5 (Cambridge, 1998).

D.E. Owen, *British Opium Policy in China and India* (New Haven, 1934).

*Papers Connected with the Settlement etc. of the Foras Lands in Bombay, BGS*, new series, No. 3 (Bombay, 1854).

Celsa Pinto, *Trade and Finance in Portuguese India: A Study of the Portuguese Country Trade, 1770-1840* (New Delhi, 1994).

C. Rajagopalan, *The Greater Bombay: A Study in Suburban Ecology* (Bombay, 1962).

Tapan Raychaudhuri and Irfan Habib eds., *The Cambridge Economic History of India*, Vol. I (Cambridge, 1982).

*Report of the Royal Commission on Opium*, Vols. VI-VII (London, 195).

John F. Richards, 'The Opium Industry in British India', *IESHR*, Vol. XXXIX, nos. 2 & 3 (2002).

Dulcinea Correa Rodrigues, *Bombay Fort in the Eighteenth Century* (Bombay, 1994).

Charles Ross ed., *Correspondence of Charles, First Marquis Cornwallis*, Vol. I, second edition (London, 1859).

G.S. Sardesai, *New History of the Marathas*, Vol. III (Bombay, 1948).

Jadunath Sarkar, *Shivaji and His Times* (New Delhi, 1973).

S.N. Sen ed., *Indian Travels of Thevenot and Careri* (Delhi, 1949).

Asiya Siddiqi, 'The Business World of Jamsetjee Jejeebhoy', Asiya Siddiqi ed., *Trade and Finance in Colonial India, 1750-1860* (Delhi, 1985).

Teotonio R. de Souza, 'Rogério de Faria: An Indo-Portuguese Trader with China Links', Artur Teodorio de Matos and Luis Filipe F.R. Thomaz, ed., *As Relações entre a Índia Portuguesa, a Ásia do Sudleste, e o Extremo Oriente* (Macao/Lisbon, 1993).

O.H.K. Spate and A.T.A. Learmonth, *India and Pakistan: A General and Regional Geography*, third edition (London, 1969).

Lakshmi Subramanian, 'Bombay and the West Coast in the 1740s', *IESHR*, Vol. XVIII, no. 2 (1981).

—, 'Banias and the British: The Role of Indigenous Credit in the Process of Imperial Expansion in Western India, in the Second Half of the Eighteenth Century', *MAS*, Vol. XXI, no. 3 (1987).

W.H. Sykes, *On the Census of the Islands of Bombay and Colabah* (Bombay, 1852).

Jean Baptiste Tavernier, *Travels in India by Jean Baptiste Tavernier*, tr. V. Ball, Vol. I (London, 1889).

Gillian Tindall, *City of Gold: The Biography of Bombay* (London, 1982).

M. Torri, 'Trapped inside the Colonial Order: The Hindu Bankers of Surat and their Business World during the Second Half of the Eighteenth Century', *MAS*, Vol. XXV, no. 2 (1991).

D.E. Wacha, *Shells from the Sands of Bombay* (Bombay, 1920).

F. Warden, *Report on the Landed Tenures of Bombay*, *BGS*, new series, No. 64 (Bombay, 1861).

George Watt, *A Dictionary of the Economic Products of India*, Vol. VI, 1, reprint (London, 1972).

J.Y. Wong, 'British Annexation of Sind in 1843: An Economic Perspective', *MAS*, Vol. XXXI, no. 2 (1997).

# ABBREVIATIONS

| | |
|---|---|
| BCA | *Bombay Calendar and Almanac* |
| BCGD | *Bombay Calendar and General Directory* |
| BGS | *Selections from the Records of the Bombay Govt.* |
| CM | Correspondência de Macau |
| XCHR | Xavier Centre of Historical Research |
| EPW | *Economic and Political Weekly* |
| GSAP | Goa State Archives |
| GSR | Grain Scarcity Records |
| HD | Home Department |
| IESHR | *The Indian Economic and Social History Review* |
| JMA | Jardine Matheson Archives |
| MAS | *Modern Asian Studies* |
| MSAM | Maharashtra State Archives |
| NAI | National Archives of India |
| SRBC | Separate Revenue Branch Consultations |

# APPENDIX - A

## Extract from a letter of Jamsetjee Jejeebhoy
## addressed to William Jardine

*[The following extract from a letter written by Jamsetjee Jejeebhoy to William Jardine[1] is representative of the extensive correspondence between Jamsetjee and Jardine Matheson and Co. and/or its predecessor companies. Jardine was at this time a partner in Magniac and Co., which he had joined in 1825. A large part of what was a voluminous correspondence has survived in the form of letterbooks maintained at both ends: the Jamsetjee Jejeebhoy Letterbooks (Mumbai University Library) and the Bombay Correspondence of Jardine Matheson/Yrissari and Co. (1821-27)/Charles Magniac (1820-25)/ Magniac and Co.[2] (Jardine Matheson Archives). The regular exchange of letters between Jamsetjee Jejeebhoy on the one hand and Jardine and Matheson on the other, especially from the 1820s to the 1840s, sheds light on almost all aspects of the opium trade between Bombay and China. As may be gathered from the present example these letters touched upon a variety of issues related to the opium trade—bids at the East India Company's Malwa opium auctions at Bombay; state of the Daman opium market; opium prices at Calcutta; problems of remittance from China to India; particulars of consignments and shipments; and opium transactions of prominent dealers. The transactions of Indian opium dealers were interwoven with those of private European traders.*

*Among other things this letter highlights the serious problem of remittance of profits, from China to Bombay, faced by indigenous opium dealers. As has been pointed out by Siddiqi, Indian opium exporters were perpetually at a disadvantage in the China market because of the hardships they faced in repatriating their earnings back to India.[3] There were primarily two means of remitting opium profits back to Bombay, bills of exchange and bullion. Bills were regarded as a better method of remittance as they were comparatively safer and the exchange was more favourable. The most sought-after bills, till 1833, were those issued by the Company on Calcutta or on the court of directors in London. Agency houses in China could deposit their cash returns with the Company's treasury in Canton and have bills issued against these. The Company used these deposits for its tea and silk investments (the Company's exchange facilities for remittance through its Canton treasury were no longer available following the Charter Act of 1833 which brought to an end its China monopoly). There were, besides, private bills issued by British financial or banking concerns, and American bills. The Company's bills were virtually paper money and therefore much in demand. There was a regular market for them in Bombay, which made it easy for the exporters to encash them. The bills on London had a greater demand, as they were required by European individuals and firms to remit funds from India to Britain. The Company's bills were not easy to obtain as their availability was much less than the demand. Hence Jamsetjee's specific request for them in this letter. Indeed Jamsetjee signs off the letter by repeating the request so as to make sure that Jardine did not miss its import: 'If you wished to assist I beg you will subscribe first in the Bill on Court of Directors…'. Later in the same year he asked Jardine to 'secure some of the United States Bills as soon as the Americans arrive at your place'.[4] After 1833 remittance for Indians became even more difficult and their dependence on private British and American bills increased. Siddiqi lists the various expedients and cumbersome procedures that Bombay exporters such as Jamsetjee Jejeebhoy had to resort to for having their profits remitted to them. Delays were costly especially if one was operating with short-term credit. The fall of several American financial concerns in 1837 due to overspeculation led to a further crisis by the end of the 1830s.[5]*

*The grammatical peculiarities of the letter are due to its being a copy of the draft (draft translation?) from which the fair version would have been prepared by someone with a better knowledge of the language.]*

O[riginal] P[er] Good Success[6]
D[uplicate] P[er] Cornwallis[7]

Bombay 1 February 1826

Private

My dear Jardine,

You will blame me for venturing in Malwa by paying such high prices the cause of which I must mention you by this conveyance to convince you that it was not in my intention nor the

House[']s[.][8] [A]s I have seen your House[']s letter to purchase
some quantity and then limittation [sic][,][9] also your concluding
part of your letter to leave something to the House[.] [Magniac
and Co.] [U]nder this circumstances myself and Mr. De Vitre[10]
consulted to buy jointly including your order that is to say if should
go from 15 to 1600 Rs p[er] chest Mr De Vitre should have 150
chests for himself and 100 chests for your House and I have 300
chests[,] and if at 1700 Rs Mr De Vitre have only 100 chests and
your House 50 chests and myself and my friends 250 chests[.]
Accordingly I have employed Capt. Frith[11] to bid for me and I
have given authorize in writing where I not mention any prices
for as I see Capt. Frith's opinion was very low and I afraid to
mention how far to go but hinted I will be at sale room at 1 : o
clock[.] If I see any wrong I will stop this business settled[.] [O]n
Monday 16th January, I was at my office when I heard one lot
been marked down Capt Frith 1700 Rs. I proposed to go at sale
room[,] as soon I reaching I heard they bidding with M/s Forbes
& Co's Parsee [agent] and boughted 10 Lots averaging 2300 Rs[.]
[I]mmediately send a word to stop of Buying any more[.][12] [T]he
moment I arrived I wished to see Mr. De Vitre and [the auction
room] was so crowded of people I could not able to see him. As I
thought best have some more [bids?] to bring the average less
[i.e. down][,] on this views I made sign to Capt Frith bid M/s
Forbes['] people and got about 57[67?] lots averaging 2020 Rs.
Mr. De Vitre when heard this being done and very much annoyed
was not his intention to pay so high prices and declined of keeping
any portion with me[.] [H]owever at last we arranging to send
180 chests of opium on joint account [consigned] to your
respectable House[,] 150 chests p[er] Good Success and 30 chests
p[er] Cornwallis to follow in week after[,] one third for our friends
and 2/3 for my House and leave the rest for your good and

experienced Judgement to do the best for our Interest[.] The quantity [sic; quality?] are indeed very good to all the preceding season[,] however you will find [i.e. you can confirm this] on examination with Chinese[,] and I have great confidence on you that you will save us from Loss and leaved [sic] entirely to your goodselves to do the best you can for our Interest and carry the Net proceed to our account as above stated. ...

M/s Calvo & Co.[13] send 3 Lacs of D[olla]rs to M/s Forbes & Co. for purchase of Malwa opium which they accordingly boughted and 100 chests send p[er] Good Success and similar quantity per Cornwallis. M/s Pereira & Co[14] also send to Sir Roger [de Faria] about 1 Lac of Dollars for this purpose and 52 chests[15] going by present conveyance[,] [and] 25 chests for Capt. Gover and 20 chests to M/s Russell & Co[16] and about 60 chests to my agent on a/c of different of our office people[,] together 487 chests on Board and I think about 300 chests will come per Cornwallis as I have arranged with Mr James Forbes to prevent by [sic] receiving some from Petty Persons in Bazar .... [17]

The Bengal 2nd sale[18] averaging 2587 [Rs] ...

Demaun [Daman[19]] opium will come 300 to 400 chests for certain but the other [additional quantity?] our friend Motychand [Motichund Amichund] trying to bring at Demaun is very doubtful[20] but not exceed altogether 7 to 800 chests[21] as we heard great obstacle and danger on the road[22] which will let you know by other conveyance.

You will [be] surprize[d] that all the China goods[23] are nothing but lossing [sic] concern[,] even Spanish Dollars[24] but if you can procure some Bills on Court of Directors will suit our purpose very well or some sycee silver[25] [which] always fetch 102 to 102½ [Rs] p[er] 100 Tollas and if you paid 6% or little more [insurance charges?] still better than Spanish Dollars.

Or if you can procure some independent Dollars[26] by discount as before will answer well however leaved this entirely to your judgement[,] insuring always at your place.

Our Good Success have ordered to Dispatch soon from China[,] if you can conveniently made [sic] some remittance to our care as suggested above will do great favor and at same time beg your advancing us any sum the Interest should be as moderate, as I am old Friend of the House [Magniac and Co., but personally of Jardine] and always wellwisher of your welfare.

I think I said too much at present but wishing you good health and prosperity may attend your wishes[.] If you wished to assist I beg you will subscribe first in the Bill on Court of Directors otherwise I am afraid my not stop of receiving any more [sic].

*Jamsetjee Jejeebhoy*

To William Jardine Esq.
Canton

P.S. I have find that late Mr Ch[arles] Magniac[27] have obtained 2 shares for me in the Canton office and I have accordingly given risk in this office in Bombay and beg you will give a portion occasionally in my name to that office and oblige.

NB. You will perceive our letter No 2 to your House with enclosures one from M/s Ritchie Stewart & Co of this place and I hope you will attend personally to the wishes therein contained and which I think will do well if you can procure and forward direct to their agent as desired and oblige.

Enclosure:

My Dear Sir,

I intend to send 30 chests more opium on Board the Good Success today and will thank you to send me an order for that quantity.

I should be glad also to know how many chests you send yourself by the Success that we may advise our friends that no small lots[28] have been sent on nor will be by the Cornwallis to interfere with them in the market[.] I hope you have retained a portion of yours for the Cornwallis.[29]

*James Forbes*
31 January 1826

To
Jamsetjee Jejeebhoy

\*

Lots of opium on Board the *Good Success*

| | | |
|---|---|---|
| 150 | chests consigned to | M/s Magniac & Co. |
| 20 | -do- | Russell & Co. |
| 75 | -do- | Saboodeen Guttay |
| 25 | -do- | Cursetjee Limjee |
| 100 | -do- | Calvo & Co. |
| 10 | -do- | Framjee Ruttunjee |
| 52 | -do- | J.J. Ferreira Veiga |
| 25 | -do- | Capt. John Gover |

447[30]

| | | |
|---|---|---|
| | | Singapore[31] |
| 30 | -do- | G. McKenzie or eventually to David & Co. |

| 10 | -do- | Ismail Feckariah – Sabodeen Guttay |

1 February 1826
*Jamsetjee Jejeebhoy*

## Notes

1 Letter dated 1 February 1826, NAI, Jamsetjee Jejeebhoy Letterbooks, microfilm, reel 1.

2 See chapter II, note 64, above.

3 Siddiqi, 'Business World', pp.202-208.

4 Letter dated 9 October 1826, NAI, Jamsetjee Jejeebhoy Letterbooks, microfilm, reel 1.

5 Siddiqi, 'Business World', pp.204-205. See also Cheong, *Mandarins and Merchants*, pp. 6-8.

6 Owned by Jamsetjee Jejeebhoy.

7 Owned by Motichund Amichund.

8 This refers perhaps to Remington Crawford and Co, Bombay.

9 I.e. in terms of price.

10 On behalf of Remington Crawford and Co..

11 Capt. A.G. Frith had been the commander of the brig Caçador in 1825 that carried Motichund Amichund's consignment of Malwa opium (Bombay and Daman). See chapter II, above. Capt. Frith was one of the several 'free mariners' who were licensed by the company's court of directors to officer 'country ships' in Asia. The 'free mariners' at Bombay were involved in the opium trade as well. On 'free mariners' see Anne Bulley, *The Bombay Country Ships*, 1790-1833 (Richmond, 2000), pp.207, 209.

12 The average price of Malwa opium auctioned by the company at Bombay in 1825 (2500 chests) was Rs.971.45 (Board of Customs, Salt and Opium, 26 August 1825, NAI, SRBC, 14/15 September 1825). The present letter indicates that opium dealers at Bombay were aware that prices in 1826 would be much

higher than in the previous season, but were not prepared for such a steep rise. The increase in prices was partly due to a shortfall in production caused by adverse weather conditions in Malwa (See, Farooqui, *Smuggling as Subversion*, p.64, Table 1). The average price of Malwa opium auctioned at Bombay in 1826 was Rs.1878 per chest, almost double the figure for 1825. The average for the January sales was Rs.1988 (1250 chests), which came down to Rs.1768 (1250 chests) in March. The letter points towards leading exporters combining in an attempt to lower the company's prices. However, it is significant that the average price of Malwa opium chests auctioned at Calcutta in 1826 was much lower, Rs.1418 (1500 chests). This justified bringing a larger number of chests to Bombay as compared to Calcutta. The Company had auctioned 2500 chests at Calcutta in 1823 and 1824, respectively, reserving only 1500 chests for Bombay in each year. From 1825 onwards the proportion was reversed (Statement dated 9 August 1826, NAI, SRBC, 8/7 September 1826). After 1826 the entire stock of the East India Company's Malwa opium was auctioned at Bombay, and the Calcutta sales (of Malwa opium) were discontinued. Since higher prices could be realized at Bombay, it made no sense to carry a portion of Malwa opium chests to Calcutta. Moreover, given the large demand for Malwa opium at Bombay, 4000 chests could be easily absorbed by dealers at this port. The Bombay government had stated in 1826 that 'It must be admitted that sufficient capital exists in Bombay to purchase annually the Company's investment of 4,000 chests at fair prices, whilst it is equally obvious that ... the measure of holding all their sales of Malwa opium in Bombay will materially benefit the Company, to say nothing of the blow it must give to the Demaun trade...' (Francis Warden, 'Minute' dated 11 August 1826, NAI, SRBC, 7/7 September 1826).

[13] D.L. Calvo and Co., Portuguese firm of Macao. Cf. Lembrança, 6.12.1828, Monções do Reino, 205-B, fol.702, enclosure 9.

[14] Portuguese firm of Macao.

[15] In the books of Roger de Faria and Co. these 52 chests are stated to be on account of the Macao Portuguese firm of Joaquim Jose Ferreira Veiga. They were valued at Rs.1,08,777. What Jamsetjee probably means is that dollars worth about one lakh rupees had been sent to Bombay. Lembrança, 6.12.1828, Monções do Reino, 205-B, fol.702, enclosure 9 (on dollars see notes 22 and 24 below). This document, which is extracted from the books of Roger de Faria and Co., was intended to establish that in the late 1820s a large number of Macao Portuguese firms had been regularly instructing de Faria to carry their Malwa opium to Lintin, thereby undermining the position of Macao. The shift to Lintin and Whampoa eventually led to the decline of the opium trade at Macao.

[16] During the late 1820s and early 1830s Russell and Co. emerged as the leading American firm engaged in smuggling opium into China. It collaborated closely with Jardine Matheson. Cheong has remarked that after 1833 'the two British houses of Jardine, Matheson & Co. and Dent, Whiteman & Co. and the American agency of Russell & Co. virtually inherited the [company's Canton] Committee's financial and commercial responsibilities'. Cheong, *Mandarins and Merchants*, p.8.

[17] Obviously the big players, who virtually constituted a syndicate, were keen to monopolize the opium trade to the extent possible by excluding 'petty' merchants who tended to lower prices through their small-scale operations: 'the consignments of Petty merchants I fear do harm by forcing the market' (Jamsetjee to Jardine, 11 March 1826, NAI, Jamsetjee Jejeebhoy Letterbooks, microfilm, reel 1).

[18] East India Company's Bengal opium ('Benaras' and 'Patna') auction at Calcutta, as distinct from Malwa opium sales at Calcutta.

[19] The Portuguese rendering was Damão (pronounced Damâon). In documents written in English, Demaun thus became the standard spelling for Daman.

[20] Motichund Amichund was the only Bombay opium dealer of some consequence who was engaged in directly smuggling opium from Malwa to Daman, via Karachi.

[21] Eventually a little over 1600 chests of Daman opium were estimated to have made their way to China in 1826. See chapter II, Table 3. It should be borne in mind that some of the Daman opium was of inferior quality and therefore fetched much lower prices than company Malwa.

[22] This refers to the smuggling route via Pali and Karachi.

[23] E.g. tea, silk and dyes.

[24] Spanish (silver) Colonial dollars, minted from American silver, became the major currency for international trade in southeast Asia from the late eighteenth century onwards.

[25] Chinese silver ingots.

[26] Silver coins, other than Spanish dollars, which circulated in China at this time, as for instance Mexican dollars issued after Mexico gained independence in 1821.

[27] Charles Magniac had died in 1825, following which the firm was renamed Magniac & Co.

28   Cf. note 17, above.

29   The Cornwallis carried 260 chests of opium (Jamsetjee informed Jardine with satisfaction 'glad to intimate you she only carry 260 chests for China'), of which Jamsetjee's consignment amounted to 35 chests. Letter dated 8 February 1826, NAI, SRBC, Jamsetjee Jejeebhoy Letterbooks, microfilm, reel 1.

30   There is a discrepancy in the total, which comes to 457. The error seems to be in figures pertaining either to chests consigned to Saboodeen Guttay, or Cursetjee Limjee, or Framjee Ruttunjee, details of which are not provided in the main text of the letter. The overall total comes to 487, which is the same as that mentioned by Jamesetjee in the main text.

31   These chests were also for the China market.

# APPENDIX – B

## The Famine of 1803 and Speculation in Foodstocks

The pattern of Bombay's intercourse as it had developed by the beginning of the nineteenth century is perhaps best illustrated by the contrast between the situation in Bombay on the one hand and the Deccan and Konkan on the other during the famine of 1803.[1] While shortages overtook the Deccan and Konkan, Bombay was in a position to support a growing population that flocked to the city to seek food and employment there in the wake of the famine.[2] A perusal of records pertaining to this period, especially for the year 1804, leaves one in no doubt that by the early nineteenth century Bombay had an extensive sea-borne trading network for supply of foodgrains to it. The Konkan was one of the major sources for the supply of grain to Bombay by the middle of the eighteenth century.[3] However, Bombay's connections permitted it to tap alternative sources further afar with the help of a merchant class capable of handling a considerable trade in grain. This merchant class already included a number of Indians trading on their own account.

It is not surprising that Forbes and Co. and Bruce, Fawcett and Co. should have been at the forefront of those who contracted to supply grain to Bombay during the famine. These two firms had been in existence since the last quarter of the eighteenth century and worked in close alliance with each other during the early nineteenth century.[4] Their connections and influence with the Bombay government are well known.[5] They were therefore able to wangle several tenders for providing grain to Bombay. We know that in 1804 Forbes and Co. had got at least one contract for 10,000 bags of rice (1 bag = 168 lbs.) to be shipped from Bengal.[6] In August 1804 a lengthy correspondence ensued between Forbes and Co., Bruce, Fawcett and Co., and some other firms and the Bombay government over the question of raising the price of rice originally stated in their tender.[7] Initially, these firms had undertaken to supply rice at Rs.7 per bag. In August 1804 the Bombay government agreed to a price of Rs.9 per bag, though merchants kept complaining that the price might rise to over Rs.12 per bag.[8] It was reported that the prices at Calcutta had been rising due to the increase in demand at Bombay,[9] which is significant being indicative of the orientation of the market. Sea-borne trade made the economic integration of Bombay with Calcutta much easier. The cost for transporting grain from Calcutta to Bombay was estimated to be four rupees per bag, for a ship-load of 10,000 bags.[10] Among the Indian merchants involved in this trade we have reference to Nusserwanji Manockji of Bombay who had been commissioned by Dorabji Byramji of Calcutta to dispose 29,000 bags of rice.[11] Nusserwanjee Manockji belonged to the Wadia family.

Not without reason then a large number of people sought refuge in Bombay, where food was more easily available as was some sort of poor relief and employment through public works like road construction.[12] Speculation in foodstocks, and adulteration, were also rampant.[13]

# Notes

[1] Among the causes of the Great Famine of 1803 in the Konkan was the partial failure of rains in 1802 and a more complete failure in 1803. See Campbell, *Materials*, Vol.III, p.522.

[2] Cf. *Imperial Gazetteer*, Vol.VIII, p.407.

[3] By the 1740s the Company was regulating the grain trade of the Konkan to meet Bombay's growing demands. Cf. Lakshmi Subramanian, 'Bombay and the West Coast in the 1740s', *IESHR*, Vol. XVIII, 2 (1981), p.216.

[4] Douglas, *Bombay and Western India*, Vol.I, p.244.

[5] Ibid., p.242; also Nightingale, *Trade and Empire*, pp.24-5.

[6] R. Henshaw, customs master, Bombay, to J.A. Grant, secretary, Bombay Govt., 20 August 1804, MSAM, GSR, Diary 319.

[7] Letter to Bombay Govt., 22 August 1804, MSA, GSR, Diary 319.

[8] Ibid.

[9] Ibid.

[10] Ibid.

[11] Letter to Henshaw, 23 August 1804, MSA, GSR, Diary 319.

[12] Cf.MSA, GSR, Diary 317-322, September 1803 to June 1806.

[13] Letter to Grant, 17 July 1804, MSA, GSR, Diary 319.